# Whatever Happened to the Twelve Apostles?

## ELVA SCHROEDER

Even Before
Publishing

Whatever Happened to the Twelve Apostles?
© Elva Schroeder 2010
jimelva@ozemail.com.au

Published by Even Before Publishing; Christian books by Wombat Books.
P. O. Box 1519, Capalaba Qld 4157
www.evenbeforepublishing.com
www.wombatbooks.com.au

Second Edition
Original edition published by Peacock Publications
ISBN: 1876087684
Cover painted by Muriel Stevenson

All scripture refernces are taken from the New International Version of the Bible, published
by Zondervan Publishing House (1996) and are used by permission.

Design and layout by Even Before Publishing

ISBN: 978-1-921633-17-1

National Library of Australia Cataloguing-in-Publication entry
Author:        Schroeder, Elva.
Title:         Whatever happened to the twelve apostles? / Elva Schroeder.
Edition:       2nd ed.
ISBN:          9781921633171 (pbk.)
Notes:         Includes bibliographical references.
Subjects:      Bible. N.T.--Biography.
               Apostles--Biography.
Dewey Number:   225.9

*Whatever Happened to the Twelve Apostles?* Good question. From the New Testament alone it is not easy to know. In this engaging and readable book, Elva Schroeder uncovers their hidden stories and unearths some surprising answers. You'll never think about the Twelve the same way again.

*Dr Barry Chant, Author and Founding President, Tabor College*

At Pentecost, different ethnic groups heard the Spirit of God speaking in their own languages. Historical records tell us that the apostles split into groups and followed not long after. This absorbing and carefully-researched book tracks the apostles as they move from country to country spreading the Good News. An inspiring and very different perspective on the early days of Christianity - un-put-downable!

*Anne Hamilton, president of Omega Writers*

This book is one of the best and most concise attempts at describing what happened to the personalities of the New Testament. The lives of these men present us with a challenge for our own lives and perhaps even more importantly for our children. In addition, you will be fascinated by the last two chapters, Who were the Seventy and Church Fathers and Historians, that take us beyond the Apostles to a broader reference and for me creates greater fascination. Reading this book is an enriching experience for all Christians

*Peter Frogley, Director and Founder of Light Educational Ministries*

There are two erroneous impressions concerning Jesus' twelve apostles which hold sway in the modern world. The first is that what we know of Jesus was written later by those who were not eye-witnesses of his life, death and resurrection. Elva's work demonstrates that the birth of Christianity was in the dynamic witness of real people who testified to 'that which we have heard which we have seen with our eyes ... and have touched with our hands concerning the Word of life.

The second is that the majority of the disciples faded out, leaving the apostolic work to Paul and his companions. Elva demonstrates that all of the apostles, Matthias replacing Judas, spent the rest of their lives testifying to their personal experience of Jesus Christ. Eleven were martyred for their testimony and none recanted the veracity of their witness. Elva's work is timely and very helpful in this current sceptical and dismissive age

*Rod James, Uniting Church Minister of the Word*

# Acknowledgements

Firstly, I would like to thank my husband Jim for his unwavering support and encouragement over my more than twenty years of research and preparation for this book.

I would also like to thank my son Brian for borrowing or buying numerous reference books for my use.

Also I would like to thank the following people for permission to quote from their books:

Tyndale House, The Search for the Twelve Apostles by William Steuart McBirnie,

Penguin UK, The History of the Church from Christ to Constantine by Eusebius, translated by G A Williamson,

Oxford University Press, The Apocryphal New Testament,

Covenant Publishing Co Ltd, for books by Robert Stoker, George Jowett, R W Morgan, Gladys Taylor and J W Taylor.

# Also by Elva Schroeder

Outback Evangelist
Doctor Sahib
The Secret Cavern
Cathy

These are available through the author:
jimelva@ozemail.com.au

# Contents

# INTRODUCTION

Have you ever wondered just what the twelve apostles did after the excitement of the Day of Pentecost died down?

In the early chapters of Acts it seems as if Peter and John were the only ones doing anything much for the Lord while the rest of the apostles just tagged along, attending prayer meetings and holding house meetings. Stephen and Philip, two of the newly-elected deacons, appear to have had a far greater public ministry than most of the twelve.

Then in 44AD, fourteen years after the ascension of Christ, James[1] the brother of John, was beheaded by King Herod. One of the inner three who had received special training from Jesus, James seems to have accomplished hardly anything for the Lord before his life was cruelly snuffed out.

When Peter was miraculously released from prison a short time later, we read that he 'left for another place'. From then on we catch only brief glimpses of him in the New Testament. Practically nothing is related about the rest of the apostles until we find John on the Isle of Patmos in the book of Revelation.

It would appear that all the special training Jesus had given these twelve was virtually wasted, with the burden of taking the gospel to the ends of the earth now resting primarily on the shoulders of Paul and his companions.

Yet Jesus must have considered the original twelve, with the exception of Judas Isariot, extremely important to the future of His kingdom on earth. Before selecting them, He spent the whole night in prayer, seeking the Father's will in the matter. There would have been several hundred followers from whom Jesus could have chosen, but He picked these twelve, knowing Judas would ultimately betray Him.

## THRONES

Towards the end of his ministry Jesus informed the twelve[2] that in His future kingdom, they would 'sit on twelve thrones, judging the twelve tribes of Israel'.

Then in the book of Revelation, John saw the names of the twelve apostles - Matthias apparently taking the place of Judas - written on the twelve foundations of the New Jerusalem.

Surely each of the twelve apostles must have done something remarkable to warrant these great honours.

## GREAT COMMISSION

After His resurrection, on a hillside in Galilee and again in the upper room, Jesus gave his disciples the Great Commission.[3]  They were to "go into all the world and preach the gospel to all creation, preaching repentance and forgiveness of sins and making disciples of all nations, baptising them in the name of the Father, and of the Son and of the Holy Ghost, teaching them to obey everything He had commanded them."

Then  just before He was  taken up into heaven, Jesus  told His disciples that after the Holy Spirit came upon them, they were to be His witnesses "in JERUSALEM and in all JUDEA and in SAMARIA and to the ENDS OF THE EARTH."

So did the twelve actually fulfil the great expectations Jesus had for them?  The last verse of Mark's gospel,[4] backed up by the writer to the Hebrews, seems to indicate that they did.   Whether the last few verses of Mark's gospel were written by Mark himself or by Aristion, a disciple of Jesus and later Bishop of Smyrna, the message is still clear.  The disciples are said to have "gone out and preached everywhere, and the Lord worked with them and confirmed His word by the signs that accompanied it."

Justin Martyr, writing around 150 AD, also states that the apostles "went to every race of men and taught these things."

To find out just where each one went and what they actually did, however, is quite a challenge.

In an effort to piece together an outline of  where each apostle traveled in their service for the Lord, we have to turn to scraps of information in the writings of the early church fathers, along with generally accepted traditions and at times the recorded history of a church in a given area.

Protestants have often rejected some early accounts of the activities of the apostles as many of these stories emphasise Patron Saints, Patriarchs, bones or other relics, and at times the worship of Mary. This would apply especially to many of the rather fanciful stories in the Apocryphal New Testament.

Yet however far fetched some of these stories  may seem, it is probable that there is a basis of fact, based on oral tradition, underlying many of them. Where we find references to an apostle ministering in a certain place in the writings of reputable church historians, we can cautiously fill in their histories with some details from these accounts where they seem appropriate.

## BISHOPS

Another problem for some is the constant reference in early church writings to noted Christians as 'Bishop'[5] of a particular church.

In the New Testament we read that Paul ordained elders, bishops or presbyters, along with deacons in all the churches he established.

Elder was a Hebrew term which originated back in the early days of the nation of Israel and had carried over to the leadership of the synagogues.

A certain number of elders was responsible for each synagogue, with a leading elder or rabbi elected as 'ruler of the synagogue'. Jairus held this position in the synagogue at Capernaum.

Bishop - or episkopos - was a Greek word and was originally used to describe the same office as elder in the non-Jewish churches. But whereas elder denoted age as well as rank, the term bishop described the position of overseer, regardless of age.

Thus, in Paul's letter to Timothy, he urges the younger man not to feel inferior because of his age, but to accept the position conferred upon him by the laying on of hands of the presbyters or elders. Eusebius names Timothy and Titus as bishops of Ephesus and Crete respectively. Both had authority to appoint elders and deacons in the churches under their care.

Eusebius also designates James the brother of Jesus as Bishop of the Jerusalem church. James was certainly the recognised leader, with the elders and even the apostles accepting his oversight.

At a fairly early stage, it seems, one of the elders or presbyters in each church was appointed to oversee the activities of the group, with the other elders sharing the teaching ministry while the deacons served in a more practical capacity.

Where an apostle established a certain church, or ministered there for a number of years, he is often referred to as its first bishop.

Therefore, by taking note of which town or country claimed a particular apostle as its first bishop, Patron Saint, or Patriarch, or where their bones were said to be buried, along with other information, we can usually put together a reasonably comprehensive picture of their varied ministries.

## DATES

It is impossible to be dogmatic about specific dates from a distance of two thousand years. However, to try and place the activities of the apostles in a chronological framework, we need to establish a few basic, generally accepted historical dates, and build from there.

When Jesus was born[6] time was calculated in the Roman Empire from the founding of the city of Rome, known as Anno Urbis 1. In 526 AD a Scythian monk named Dionysius Exiguus was requested by the Roman Emperor Justinian to set up a new calendar dating everything from the birth of Christ. It was later discovered, however, that Dionysius had overlooked the four years that Emperor Augustus had reigned under his own name of Octavian. He had therefore placed the birth of Christ in the year Anno Urbis 753 instead of about 749 or even earlier.

When the angel appeared to Joseph in Egypt he told him it was now safe to take Mary and Jesus back to Israel as King Herod, who had sought to kill Jesus, was dead. The death of Herod is said to have been in late March or early April of 4BC.

It is considered that it would have been too cold for the shepherds, to whom the angels appeared, to be out in the fields with their sheep any later than mid November. Therefore the birth of Christ is generally thought to have occurred in late October or early November of 5BC.

As Dionysius had not made allowance for the year '0' in his calendar, this would make Jesus thirty years and a few months at the time of his baptism, probably around the traditional date of the 10th January 27AD.

Luke tells us that Jesus was 'about thirty years of age' when he began his ministry. This is generally thought to have been at the time of the Passover, 9th-11th April 27AD.    Jesus' ministry is considered to have lasted for three years, leading to His crucifixion and resurrection during the Passover celebrations of 7th - 9th April 30AD.

It is from this date that we will endeavour to establish the possible ministries of the twelve apostles.

Although specific dates are rather scarce,  an approximate date for a particular apostle's ministry in a certain place can often be arrived at by taking into account the times they are said to have worked with others.   Where dates or details seem to be contradictory, even in respected church histories, we need to line them up with other known facts and aim at the most likely scenario.

## WHEN DID THE APOSTLES LEAVE JERUSALEM?

It has often been thought that the apostles remained in Jerusalem for up to fifteen years after the resurrection. But this would mean they had totally disregarded Jesus' final instructions to them.

To try and ascertain just how soon the apostles could have left Jerusalem, we first need to establish when the stoning of Stephen[7] took place.

Eusebius states that the seven new deacons "were headed by Stephen, who was the first after the Lord - almost as soon as he was ordained...- to be put to death, stoned by the Lord's murderers."

The traditional date for the stoning of Stephen is the 26th December, but of which year is open to controversy.   Those who opt for a date of 34AD or later, have usually taken the date of the crucifixion to be 33AD.   Most others, however, seem to consider either 30 or 31AD as the most likely date, with the conversion of Saul a few months later in 31 or 32AD.

We read in Acts that as a result of the persecution of the church by Saul following the death of Stephen, the Christians, except for the apostles, were scattered throughout Judea and Samaria.

If we settle on the 26th December 31AD for the martyrdom of Stephen, then it could have been as early as February or March of 32AD that Stephen's fellow deacon, Philip, went down to Samaria and preached Christ, with amazing results.

When the news reached Jerusalem, Peter and John were sent by the other apostles to check out the situation and to pray for the new believers to receive the Holy Spirit.

The apostles had now fulfilled Christ's command to preach the gospel in JERUSALEM, JUDEA and SAMARIA, but what about the rest of the world?

## DIVIDED THE WORLD

It may have been on the return of Peter and John from Samaria that, as Eusebius, Socrates, Latourette[8] and others tell us, the apostles divided the known world into specific areas. After praying for the Lord's guidance, they drew lots to discover their respective spheres of service.

It is possible, therefore, that as early as mid-32AD many of the apostles may have set out from Jerusalem to take the message of Christ to the ends of the then known earth.

In seeming confirmation of this, when Paul visited Jerusalem around 35AD, he tells us that the only member of the twelve he saw was Peter, along with James the Lord's brother, who had been appointed leader of the church in Jerusalem.

## HOW OLD WERE THE APOSTLES?

The only apostle for whose age we have any definite details is John.[9]

Generally acknowledged as the youngest of the twelve, John would nevertheless have been at least thirty when Jesus sent the apostles out two by two in 29AD to preach and heal. Under God's instructions the Levites were not to commence their duties before the age of thirty, and the Jews generally did not consider a man mature enough to be a teacher or rabbi before this age. John the Baptist and Jesus each waited until after their thirtieth birthday before beginning their respective ministries.

John is the only one of the twelve considered to have died a natural death, and he is thought to have lived to almost one hundred years of age.

## DOMITIAN

In the book of Revelation we find that in old age John was exiled to the barren island of Patmos for his testimony to Jesus. This was during the persecution of the church by the Emperor Domitian around 94-95 AD.

Among others who suffered under Domitian[10] at this time were his cousin, the Roman consul Titus Flavius Clemens and Clemens' wife, Flavia Domitilla. Domitian had Clemens executed for 'atheism', a common term for Christianity, and Flavia Domitilla was exiled to the small island of Pandateria, near the Bay of Naples.

Domitilla's administrator, Stephanus, was so incensed by all this, that he led a group of conspirators in assassinating the 44-year-old Domitian on the 18th September 96AD.

The new emperor, Nerva, immediately rescinded Domitian's orders, restoring Domitilla to her properties, and the apostle John to the church at Ephesus.

## DEATH OF JOHN

John is said to have resided at Ephesus for the next two years, preaching and overseeing the churches of Asia, before dying[11] peacefully on the 26th September 98AD.

Jerome writes that John served the Lord faithfully for sixty-eight years after the resurrection of Jesus, and both he and Irenaeus tell us that John lived until the time of Trajan, who was proclaimed emperor in January 98 AD.

Depending in which month John's birthday fell, the aged apostle was probably ninety-nine and some months when he died, making him approximately one year older than any given date.

Thus at the time of the resurrection, we can fairly safely conclude that John was about thirty-one years of age.

## PETER

Peter[12] is thought to have been the eldest of the twelve, judging by the way he automatically assumed leadership of the group and the fact that none of the others challenged him for it. Age was important in Jewish culture and other things being equal, would have given him the right to speak for the others. Thiede and others consider Peter was probably around seventy-five when he died in 67 AD, making him about thirty-eight at the time of the resurrection.

The rest of the twelve would most likely therefore have ranged in age between thirty-one year old John and thirty-eight year old Peter, making them all relatively young men in the prime of life.

So just where did each of these twelve apostles go to spread this new, life-changing message that the Lord Jesus had entrusted to them?

# REFERENCES

1. Acts 12:1-3, 17,  Revelation 1:9, Luke 6:12-17
2. Matthew 19:28, Luke 22:29-30, Revelation 21:14
3. Matthew 28:16-20, Mark 16:14-20, Luke 24:47-49, Acts 1:8
4. Mark 16:20, Hebrews 2:3-4, Eusebius (W) p 150,  Hunter pp 25, 53, Acts 2:43, 5:12-16.
5. Philippians 1:1, I Timothy 3:2, 4:12-14, Titus 1:5-9, Jackson pp 212-214, Eusebius (W) pp 109, 72, Acts 15:6,13,19,
6. Halley p657, Fausset p 96, IVP Bible Dictionary, Vol I pp 200-201
7. FF Bruce (NT Hist) p 22,  Keller pp 335-336, Unger (A:NT) pp 58, 60, Fausset p 284, Thompson's NIV p 1569, Scofield's conc p 42, Schaff p138, Halley pp 460, 492.
8. Eusebius (W) p 71, Fausset p 664, Halley pp 559, 567,  Acts 8:5-17
9. Eusebius (W) p 107,  Socrates EH 1:19, Latourette p 101,  James pp 365, 453,  Galatians 1:18-19
10. Fausset pp 384, 432,   Schaff pp 113, 569,  Matthew Henry p 323, Numbers 4:3, I  Chronicles 23:3,  Luke 3:1-3, 23,   Fox (B) p 10
11. McBirnie pp 112,  Revelation 1:9, Eusebius (S) p 8, Halley p 637 (Dio Casius 67:44), Thiede (L) pp 188-189
12. FF Bruce (NT Hist) p 391, Jerome pp 364-365, McBirnie pp 109,110, (Irenaeus), 113, 117(Jerome), 119 (26th Sept) Eusebius (S) p 120,  (W) p 128,    Enc Brit Vol X p 87
13. Thiede p 201

# ANDREW

One of those who receives little mention in the New Testament is Andrew.[1] His name occurs thirteen times in the gospels and Acts, where he is often designated "Simon Peter's brother", as though he wasn't important enough to stand alone. Yet the Greek name Andrew means "manly", and in many ways Andrew exhibited a quiet strength of character and purpose that were often sadly lacking in his older, more gregarious brother.

Andrew and Peter were natives of Galilee. Born in Bethsaida, they had later moved to Capernaum where the brothers shared a reasonably large house and a fishing business. Their father's name was John, and tradition tells us their mother was Johanna. The parents were apparently still living at Bethsaida.

Peter was married, with a mother-in-law and 'family' according to Clement of Alexandria, whereas Andrew appears to have remained a bachelor.

Andrew was probably around thirty-one years of age when he, Peter, John, possibly James and even Philip may have taken a consignment of Galilean fish to sell at the fish market in Jerusalem, staying overnight at John's small 'town-house'.[2]

Andrew and John are said to have been disciples of John the Baptist, and the two probably went to hear him preach whenever they were in Jerusalem. This day, as they stood among the crowd at Bethany across the river Jordan from Jericho, John suddenly paused in his preaching. Pointing dramatically at Jesus as He walked by, John declared with deep conviction, "Look, the Lamb of God who takes away the sin of the world."

Immediately Andrew and John left the Baptist and followed Jesus, perhaps to a cave among the rocky hills on the far side of the Jordan. John tells us that it was about the tenth hour, or 10am Roman time,

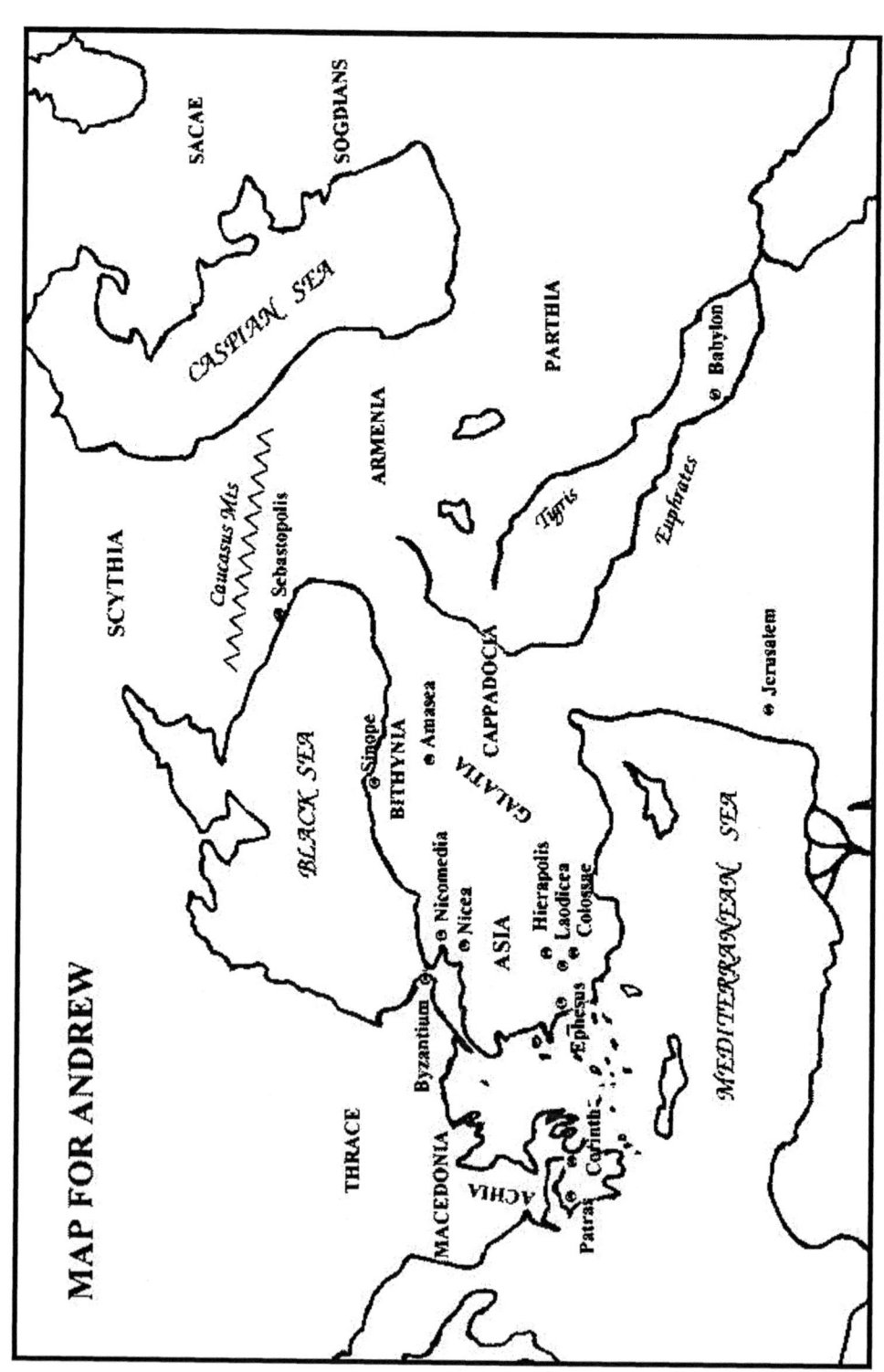

# MAP FOR ANDREW

SACAE

SOGDIANS

CASPIAN SEA

SCYTHIA

PARTHIA

⊕ Babylon

ARMENIA

Caucasus Mts

Tigris

Euphrates

● Sebastopolis

⊕ Jerusalem

BLACK SEA

⊕ Sinope

⊕ Amasea

CAPPADOCIA

BITHYNIA

GALATIA

THRACE

Byzantium ⊕

⊕ Nicomedia

⊕ Nicea

ASIA

Hierapolis ⊕

⊕ Laodicea

● Colossae

MACEDONIA

⊕ Ephesus

MEDITERRANEAN SEA

ACHIA

Patras Corinth

and says they spent the rest of that day talking with Jesus. Whatever was discussed during those memorable hours, Andrew, at least, was firmly convinced that he had finally found the Messiah for whom all Israel had so long been waiting.

His first act, probably the following day, was to bring his brother Simon   to Jesus. The fact that Simon didn't argue or ridicule Andrew's announcement that he had found the Messiah, seems to indicate that for all his brashness, Simon genuinely respected his younger brother's opinion and integrity.

## PROTOCLETE

The early church designated Andrew the Protoclete[3] or First-Called, and he seems never to have wavered in his belief that Jesus was indeed the promised Messiah.

We can only wonder at his feelings, therefore, when Jesus chose Peter, James and John as His inner circle of friends while Andrew, brother of Peter and close friend of John, was left out.  A lesser man may have gone off in a huff but we find no indication of Andrew being anything other than loyal, faithful and supportive to both Jesus and the other disciples.

As well as bringing his brother to Jesus, Andrew was the one who brought the lad with the five loaves and two fishes to the Master, setting the scene for one of Jesus' most memorable miracles in the feeding of the five thousand on the eastern shore of the Lake of Galilee.

Then just a few days before the crucifixion, some Greeks came to Philip asking to see Jesus. Philip told Andrew and together they took the men to the Master.

Tradition suggests that Luke may have been one of those Greeks, although the Muratorian Fragment states that Luke did not see Jesus in the flesh.   If, however, Luke was one of that group, then Andrew was responsible for introducing to Jesus two men who, between them, wrote nearly half the New Testament.

Andrew was one of those in the upper room who received the Holy Spirit[4] in such a miraculous way on the Day of Pentecost.  For the next few months, along with the rest of the apostles,  Andrew would have been  kept extremely busy,  teaching the thousands of new converts, holding  communion services in various homes and generally helping to establish the young church. During this time, Luke tells us, many wonders and miraculous signs were done by the apostles, and this would certainly have included Andrew.

Then came the stoning of Stephen and the persecution of the church by Saul, causing the new converts to be scattered far and wide. Although the apostles remained in Jerusalem for a time, when they eventually divided the world between them, Andrew discovered that his new sphere of service was to be the primitive and challenging land of Scythia.

## SCYTHIA

Scythia[5] was the country to the north and east of the Black Sea, extending across to the Caucasus mountains. The people were known and feared as primitive barbarians. In Jeremiah's time they had swept down through the passes of the Caucasus and struck terror into the hearts of the peoples of South-west Asia. Relentlessly they left a scorched-earth scene of desolation wherever they went, with the inhabitants either brutally massacred or carried off as slaves.

Josephus tells us that the Scythians were little different from wild beasts. They had no alphabet so they could neither read nor write, and they had no coinage.

They were not deeply religious and preferred to put their faith in their own magicians rather than in any unseen gods. Any sorcerer who was proved wrong, was quickly put to death, whereas a god would have been harder to deal with.

Greek cities and Roman forts dotted the coast of the Black Sea with small Jewish settlements in most of them. Their inhabitants often traded with the nomadic Scythians to their mutual advantage, but the primitive, war-like tribes were universally feared and distrusted by their more civilised neighbours.

The Scythians lived in tents, moving their cattle to the best grazing lands according to the season. One of their chiefs named Scyles, however, was quite taken with the stone houses of the Greeks and had one secretly built for himself. When his bodyguard found out, they were so angered by what they considered their leader's weakness that they promptly killed him.

These, then, were the people to whom Andrew was to take the message of God's love and forgiveness. Yet this quietly dedicated apostle seems to have spent nearly twenty years labouring for Christ amongst these unlikely people. Jerome tells us that Andrew preached in the city of Sebastopolis on the eastern coast of the Black Sea.

An account of the life of Andrew in the Church of St Andrew in Patras, Greece, relates that Andrew laboured in the heavily forested foot-hills of the Caucasus mountains (present-day Georgia in Southern Russia) and that he preached to the Scythians as far as the Caspian Sea. Jerome adds that he also preached to the Sogdians and the Sacae to the east of the Caspian Sea. During this time Andrew was stoned and imprisoned and suffered much for the sake of the gospel, but through it all he remained true to the call of Christ on his life.

Because of Andrew's faithfulness, Paul, writing to the Colossians many years later, was able to say with assurance that in Christ "there is neither Greek nor Jew, ... barbarian, **Scythian,** slave nor free, but Christ is all and is in all".

For his tireless efforts in taking the gospel to these primitive people, Andrew was later recognised as the Patron Saint of Russia.

## ARMENIA AND PARTHIA

Andrew is claimed by the Armenian[6] church as being one of five apostles - along with Jude Thadddaeus, Simon the Zealot, Bartholomew and Matthias - to have preached the gospel in their country.

According to Budge, The Acts of Andrew and Bartholomew gives an account of the two apostles' mission among the Parthians. Yet no actual dates are given for Andrew's ministry in these two countries.

The best we can do, therefore, is to take into account when he is said to have been with other apostles and try to work out a possible time frame from there.

The Armenian church claims that Bartholomew spent sixteen years in all preaching the gospel in Armenia. He is said to have arrived there in 44AD. He and Jude Thaddaeus are also said to have spent the years 60 to 66AD ministering in Greater Armenia. Allowing for this latter period of six years, it seems likely that Bartholomew was in Armenia the first time from 44 to 54AD.

Andrew could therefore have joined Bartholomew in Armenia somewhere around 52AD, with the two apostles labouring together there for approximately two years.

Then around 54AD, the two probably made their way into Parthia where they spent several years working together for the cause of Christ.

It may have been in the spring of 57AD that Bartholomew then continued on along the main highway into India. He is thought to have stayed with a settlement of Jews in the vicinity of the River Ganges for about a year, winning many converts and leaving with them a copy of Matthew's gospel in Hebrew - found later by Pantaenus - before taking a ship to Egypt.

During this time Andrew apparently returned to Armenia where he spent the next few years preaching the gospel and building up the church there.

Then in early August of 59AD, it would seem that Andrew was joined by Jude Thaddaeus and Simon the Zealot. These intrepid apostles had recently escaped from the Parthian city of Suanir, where, on the 1st July, of probably 59AD, they almost lost their lives in the Lord's service.

Simon the Zealot is another of the five apostles claimed by the Armenian church to have preached the gospel in their country. Yet this seems to be the only time Simon could have ministered there, considering his well documented exploits in other places. These three apostles apparently worked together in Armenia for about six months before being joined by Bartholomew on his return from India and Egypt.

In the early spring of 60AD, Armenian church tradition tells us, Jude Thaddaeus and Bartholomew set out to spend the next six years evangelising the area of Greater Armenia.

Around this time Simon the Zealot returned to Jerusalem before heading westward again and Andrew moved on to continue his witness for the Lord in Asia Minor.

## CAPPADOCIA, GALATIA & BITHYNIA

Among those who heard the apostles praising God in their own language on the Day of Pentecost were people from Cappadocia,[7] Pontus and Asia, Phrygia and Pamphilia.

Both Peter and Paul had visited many towns in these provinces in the preceding years and Peter's first epistle, written a few years later, is addressed to the Christians there.

However, with Paul now in prison and Peter presumably in Babylon and later Rome, Andrew seems to have spent around eight years ministering throughout this region.

The apocryphal Acts of Andrew, written around 260AD and said to be based on oral tradition, gives quite a few details of the apostle's ministry during this time. Although many of the stories are rather fantastic, there may still be a basis of fact to some of them. For instance, Demetrius of Amasea is said to have had an Egyptian boy of whom he was very fond.  When the lad died of a fever, Demetrius, hearing of Andrew's miracles, came and fell at his feet and besought his help.

Andrew went to the house, preached Christ to all who had gathered, then turned to the bier and raised the boy to life.  All who witnessed this miracle believed and were baptised.

Hearing of this, Gratinus of Sinope wrote to Andrew, begging him to come and deliver his son who had been seized by a demon. Andrew went to Sinope, and after preaching to all there, delivered the boy and also healed Gratinus of  fever and his wife of dropsy. The Patras church account tells us that Andrew was almost eaten alive by cannibals during his stay at Sinope.

## EPHESUS

Around the spring of 68AD, it is thought Andrew may have visited his old friend, the apostle John, at Ephesus.[8] Un response to a divine warning, John and the local Christians had left Jerusalem for Pella on the far side of the River Jordan shortly before Jerusalem was besieged by the Romans in 66AD. John is said to have remained at Pella for about a year, visiting the churches in Parthia during this period.

Then after the deaths of Peter and Paul in Rome, traditionally believed to have occurred on the 29th June 67AD, John was encouraged to move to Ephesus. Although Timothy was pastor of the church there, it was felt that John, as one of the few remaining apostles, was needed to help oversee what was fast becoming the new centre of the Christian world.

Jerome tells us that although the gospels of Matthew, Mark and Luke were already in circulation,  John's fellow-disciples and bishops urged him to record the things he had been preaching to the believers which were not covered in the other three gospels.

Sensing a need to combat the insidious Gnosticism which was creeping into the churches of the area, the Muratorian Fragment tells us that John asked his companions to fast and pray with him for three days that God would show him what to do. "The same night," it says, "it was revealed to Andrew, one of the apostles, that John was to write all things in his own name, and they were all to certify".

Although a date of 85-90AD has generally been accepted for the writing of John's gospel, Thiede and other scholars now feel a date prior to 70AD is more likely. One reason for this is that John states, "Now there IS in Jerusalem... a pool ...called Bethesda". This, along with other landmarks mentioned by John as still existing, would most likely have been destroyed by the armies of Titus in 70AD. If this dating should be correct, then it seems Andrew may have had a part to play in the writing of yet another portion of our New Testament.

## HIERAPOLIS TO BYZANTIUM

The apostle Philip is said to have been martyred at Hierapolis,[9] some one hundred and sixty kilometers inland from Ephesus, the previous November. One of Philip's married daughters lived at Ephesus and Andrew would almost certainly have visited her during his stay there.

Leaving Ephesus, Andrew and his disciples would have made their way east along the paved Roman highway to Hierapolis. They most likely called in at Laodicea, ten kilometers south of Hierapolis, on the main trade route from Ephesus to the Euphrates.

It is thought that Philip had often ministered at Laodicea along with Epaphras who is generally considered to have founded both this church and the one at Colossae.

During his stay at Hierapolis, Andrew may also have visited Colossae, twenty-six kilometers to the south-east. Here, believers such as Philemon, Onesimus, Archippus and others would no doubt have been grieving over the deaths of the apostles Peter, Paul and Philip the previous year.

Andrew apparently remained at Hierapolis for some months, strengthening the believers and encouraging Philip's widow and two other daughters.

Stachys, mentioned by Paul in his epistle to the Romans, and claimed by Hippolytus and Dorotheus to have been one of the seventy, is said in the Acts of Philip to have carried on the work at Hierapolis after Philip's death, holding meetings in his own home.

When Andrew eventually left Hierapolis, Stachys and several other disciples accompanied him. After travelling more than three hundred and twenty kilometers north along the main Roman highway to the road-junction at Dorylaeum, they then pushed on into Bithynia.

Jewish synagogues were situated in most of the cities of this province and no doubt Andrew would have preached in all those who would accept his message. He eventually reached the town of Nicea, where, the Acts of Andrew tells us, he performed many miracles.

After witnessing these amazing happenings, the people declared, "We believe that Jesus Christ whom you preach is the Son of God."

Andrew is said to have baptised many people at Nicea and to have appointed Callistus as their first bishop.

Moving on to Nicomedia, the Acts tells us, Andrew restored a dead youth at the gates of the city. This lad became one of Andrew's disciples and travelled with him from then on.

Boarding a ship, Andrew and his companions then crossed the Hellespont to the busy port city of Byzantium. Founded in 7BC, this thriving town dominated trade along the strategic Bosphorus strait separating Asia and Europe. Renamed Constantinople, capital of the Roman Empire, by Constantine in 330AD, the city is now known as Istanbul.

The Patras church account and other sources inform us that Andrew established a strong church at Byzantium. They and Nicephorus, historian and later bishop of Byzantium, tell us that before moving on, Andrew ordained Stachys as the church's first bishop, along with other presbyters and deacons to assist him.

## MACEDONIA TO CORINTH

Nicephorus and the Patras church account then state that from Byzantium Andrew continued his journey through Thrace and Macedonia[10], preaching the gospel and healing the sick.

The Acts of Andrew gives us further details regarding this time.

One night during his stay in Macedonia, the Acts relates, Andrew had a vision that he was soon to drink the same cup of crucifixion as his brother Peter.

When Andrew told the believers they were deeply distressed, but he encouraged them with the words, "Know, beloved, that I am about to leave you, but I trust in Jesus whose word I preach, that he will keep you from evil. That this harvest which I have sown among you may not be plucked up by the enemy, that is, the knowledge and teaching of my Lord Jesus Christ.

"Pray always and stand firm in the faith, that the Lord may root out all tares of offence and gather you into his heavenly garner as pure wheat."

For five more days Andrew taught and confirmed them, then he spread his hands and prayed, "Keep, I beseech thee, O Lord, this flock which has now known thy salvation, that the wicked one may not prevail against it, but that what by thy command and my means it has received, it may be able to preserve inviolate for ever." And all responded, "Amen".

Then Andrew took bread, broke it with thanksgiving, and gave it to all, saying, "Receive the grace which Christ our Lord gives you by me his servant." After which he kissed every one and commended them to the Lord.

Andrew and his companions then departed to Thessalonica and after teaching there for two days, they continued on down through Achaia to Corinth. Here Andrew saw many turn to the Lord and is said to have wrought amazing miracles, including the opening of blind eyes.

## MARTYRED IN PATRAS

Making his way across the Corinthian Gulf Andrew eventually reached the bustling port city of Patras on the west coast of Greece.[11] Capital of Achaia, and chief port of Peloponnese, Patras had come under Roman control after the battle of Actium in 31BC. Emperor Augustus later colonized it with Roman settlers, and it eventually became a rich and prosperous city rivalling Corinth.

There are many details of what happened to Andrew during his stay in Patras. Several very wordy accounts are contained in the Acts of Andrew. They are said to have been based on a letter written by the presbyters and deacons of Achaia. The original document, however, seems to have been greatly embellished by numerous writers over the centuries.

John Fox claims to have derived his details from the writings of early church leaders such as Bernard, Cyprian and others. Over-all the story seems to be as follows.

Not long after his arrival in Patras, Andrew was approached by a Christian named Iphidamia who had been converted by a disciple named Sosias. Iphidamia told Andrew that her mistress, Maximilla, wife of Aegeas the proconsul, was very sick and had sent for him. Andrew went and prayed for Maximilla and she was instantly healed.

Shortly after this the proconsul's brother, Stratocles, arrived from Italy. One of his slaves, Aleman, whom he loved, was taken by a demon and lay foaming at the mouth. Maximilla and Iphidamia said, "Be comforted, there is here a man of God, let us send for him."

When Andrew came he took the boy by the hand and raised him whole. Then Stratocles also believed and became a Christian.

Aegeas had been away in Macedonia, but when he returned and found a great crowd, including his wife and brother, listening to Andrew preach, he became enraged and had Andrew thrown into prison. The Christians then gathered daily at the prison where Andrew continued to encourage them in their faith.

Finally, Aegeas had Andrew brought before him and threatened that if the aged apostle did not stop preaching this message, he would be fastened to a cross. Andrew replied that he would not have preached the message of the cross if he had feared the death of the cross. He then earnestly exhorted Aegeas to turn to God, the righteous Judge. At this a furious Aegeas had Andrew beaten with rods by seven lictors. Then he ordered that the apostle be taken out and crucified.

Stratocles and a large crowd of people followed, wailing and lamenting Andrew's fate. Stratocles became so incensed that he fought with the guards, tearing their clothes. Andrew remonstrated with him not to show anger, but to accept the will of God.

A cross had been set up on the sea shore. Andrew, however, protested that he was not worthy to die on the same kind of cross as his Lord, and had them fashion the wood into the shape of an X. Aegeas had ordered that Andrew be tied, not nailed, to the cross to prolong his suffering.

For three days and two nights Andrew hung there exhorting the Christians and pleading with the unsaved to turn to the Lord. The crowd, which had swelled to more than two thousand, marvelled at the wise words and radiant face of this gentle and pious white-haired man of God.

Finally, on the 30th November 69AD, at around seventy-five years of age, Andrew passed into the presence of the Lord he had served so faithfully for almost forty years.

Maximilla and Stratocles personally took the aged apostle's body down from the cross. They had it embalmed and placed in an impressive shrine nearby where it remained venerated by the local Christians for nearly three hundred years.

Because of Aegeas's brutal actions and evil manner of life, Maximilla refused to return to him, even though he promised her much. Instead she led a quiet and reverent life among the brethren, filled with the love of Christ.

Finally, in the dead of night, unknown to his household, Aegeas arose, and in anguish of soul, cast himself down from a great height and perished.

Stratocles would not touch anything that was left by Aegeas. He said, "We have no need of these things, for they are polluted. But for me, let Christ be my friend and I his servant, and all my substance I offer to him in whom I have believed." His one desire was to live according to the teachings of the 'blessed apostle' that he might one day share 'with him in the ageless and unending kingdom.'

In later years Andrew was claimed as the Patron Saint of Greece, as well as that of Russia.

Then, around 345AD, when Constantine was seeking to collect the remains of all twelve apostles for his new church at Constantinople, Regulus,[12] bishop of Patras, took some of Andrew's bones and departed on a ship heading west. He was eventually shipwrecked on the east coast of Scotland at what is now known as St Andrew's Bay, where the church of St Regulus still stands.

Some years later Andrew was also declared Patron Saint of Scotland. His white X shaped cross against a background of blue sky was ultimately adopted as the Scottish national flag.

Then in 1603 James IV of Scotland became James I of England and the bold red cross of St George of England was superimposed over the white cross and blue background of the Scottish flag. Finally, in 1801, the broken red X shaped cross of St Patrick of

Ireland was added to the flag to give us our present 'Union Jack', or Union of Jacob.

Probably the last of the twelve to suffer martyrdom, quiet, faithful Andrew outlived his more famous brother Peter by nearly two and a half years. He travelled far and suffered much in the service of his Lord. Yet he had the joy of seeing many thousands of people won to the Saviour, as well as witnessing amazing miracles of healing through his ministry.

Andrew was eventually claimed as patron saint of three greatly diverse and far flung countries.[13] His cross, rather than being an object of shame, is honoured every time a member of the British Commonwealth salutes their flag.

In reality, however, the only honour Andrew would have sought was the commendation of the Lord he had so selflessly loved and served since that first memorable day beside the River Jordan, more than forty years earlier.

## REFERENCES FOR ANDREW

1. John 1:40-42, 6:8, Fausset p 560, Mark 1:29-30, Eusebius(W) p 140, Halley p 531, McBirnie pp 46-50, Int Std Bible Enc Vol I p 122

2. John 19:27, Fausset p 384, Halley pp 465-466, Morton p 219, John 1:28-29, 35-42

3. Barclay p 38, John 6:8-14, 12:20-22

4. Acts 2:43, 5:12

5. Eusebius p 107, Halley p 310, Jeremiah 4: 6-7, 6:22-25,

6. Josephus, Against Apion 2:37, Rice pp 44,63, Barclay pp 41-42, McBirnie pp 80-84, Fox (B) p 7, Matthew Henry p 552, Latourette p 106, William Carey p 230, Colossians 3:11

7. McBirnie pp 80, 130, 200, 207, Int Std Bible Enc Vol I p 123 (Budge II, 183ff)

8. Acts 2:9-10, I Peter 1:1, 5:13, Barclay p 41, Halley p 466,

9. Unger (Dict) p 51, McBirnie p 84, James pp 338-339

10. McBirnie p 80-82, 84, Eusebius (W) p 111, Unger (A:NT) p 273, Jerome p 364, Eusebius (S) p 145, Thiede (L) pp 41, 61, (P) p 150, Abott p 223, Halley pp 528, 632, 671, Fausset pp 384-385, I Timothy 6:20, Int Std Bible Enc Vol I p 122,Vol II p 484, John 5:2, Morton p 401

11. James pp 448-450, Eusebius (W) pp 140-141, Colossians1:7-8, 4:9,12-13, Philemon 1:1-2,23, Romans 16:9, Halley p 687, Unger (A:NT) p 268, Unger (Dict) pp 51-52, 1044, Matthew Henry p 552, McBirnie pp 82, 84, Barclay p 41
12. James p 344, Unger (Dict) p 51
13. Barclay pp 42-43, McBirnie pp 80-85, Unger (Dict) pp 51-52, James pp 358-363, Fox (Z) p 3, Fox (B) pp 6-7, Enc Brit Vol VII p 799-800
14. McBirnie p82, Barclay pp 43-44
15. Barclay p 38, Ninian Hill: The Story of the Scottish Church, AD1919, Stoker pp102-104

# JUDE THADDAEUS

Jesus had told his disciples they would bear witness to him before governors and kings.[1]   It is possible that one of the lesser-known of the twelve, Jude Thaddaeus, could have been the first of the apostles to actually leave Jerusalem and  bear witness to Jesus before a foreign king.

Jerome calls him trinomius, meaning the man with three names.[2] In the lists of the apostles in the New Testament Mark calls him Thaddaeus. In the Authorised Version Matthew calls him Lebbaeus whose surname was Thaddaeus and in Luke and Acts he is called Judas the son of James.

The Gospel of the Ebionites, mentioned by Origen, states that Jude Thaddaeus (as he is generally called) was among those who received their call to follow Jesus at the Sea of Tiberius (Galilee).

In the first three gospels no other mention is made of him, but in John's gospel, at the Last Supper Judas asks Jesus the question, "But Lord, why do you intend to show yourself to us and not to the world?" John makes a particular point of stating that this Judas was not the one surnamed Iscariot.

## KING ABGAR OF EDESSA

There is a fascinating story told by Eusebius,[3] Jerome and a number of other writers concerning the early ministry of Jude Thaddaeus. Eusebius states that Jesus' miracles had become the subject of excited discussion in many lands remote from Judaea, and that many people came seeking healing from Him.

One who heard of Jesus' miracles was King Abgar Uchama, "the brilliantly successful monarch" of the Osrhoenes.

This kingdom was named after a certain Osrhoe who founded the state about 136BC. Although Osrhoe was probably of Iranian

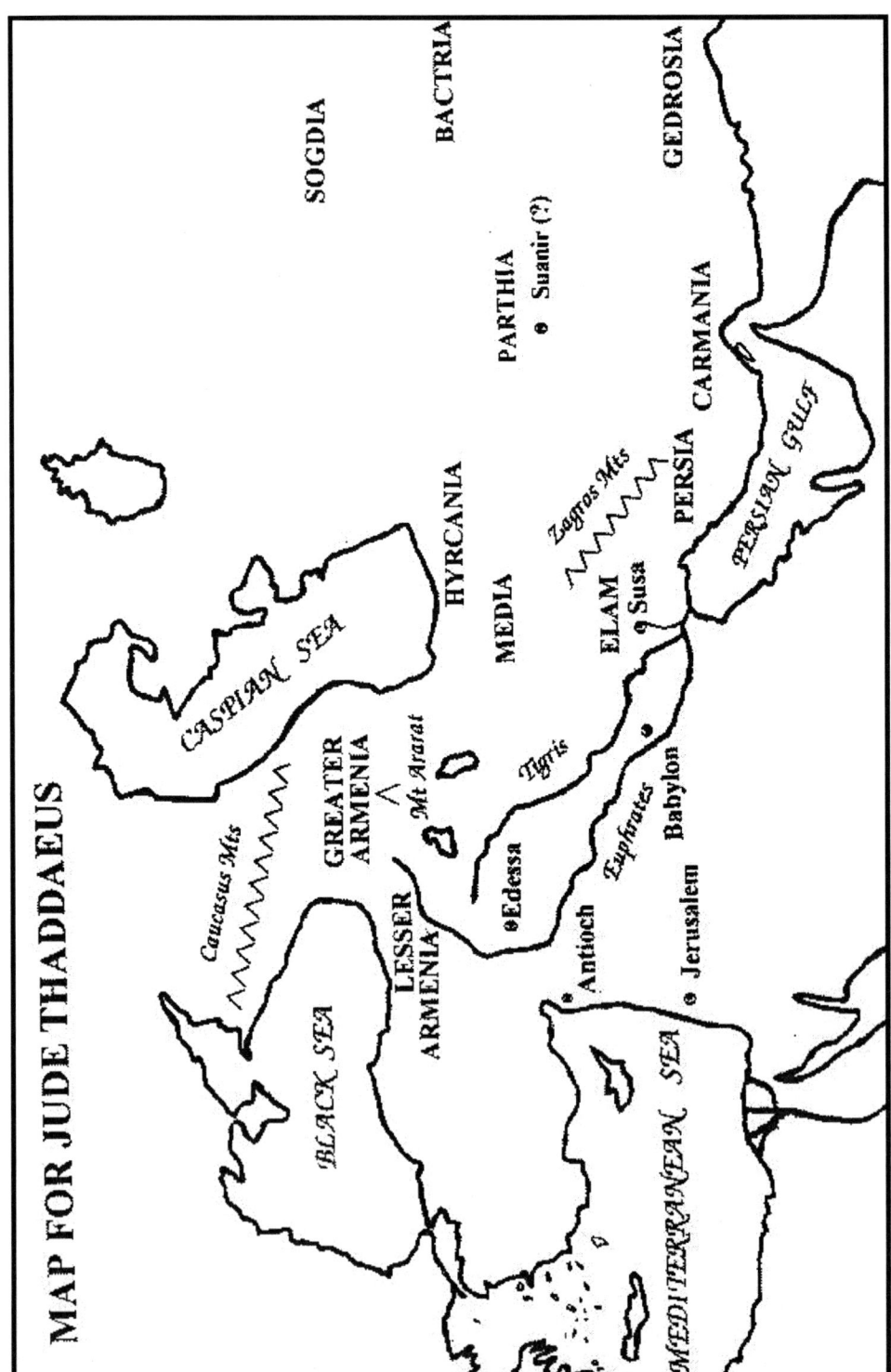

MAP FOR JUDE THADDAEUS

origin, the rulers after him were Arabs, yet the kingdom was strongly influenced by Aramaic culture.

Situated in north-western Mesopotamia between the Euphrates and Tigris rivers, the Osrhoene kingdom commanded the strategic east-west highway that followed the southern edge of the Kurdish plateau. It also controlled part of the trade route known as the old Persian Royal Road, which ran from Sardis in Anatolia to the old Persian capital of Susa, three hundred and twenty kilometers east of Babylon.

This put Osrhoene in a strong position during the wars between Rome and Parthia from the 1st century BC to the 2nd century AD leading it to form alliances with one or the other at different times.

Its main towns were Edessa, the capital, and Haran where Abraham stayed for a time after leaving Ur. Edessa, about thirty-two kilometers east of the Euphrates and two hundred and ninety kilometers north-east of Antioch, was built on a steep bluff above a valley in the fertile plain of Haran. Ringed by limestone hills on three sides, with a swift stream flowing through the walled town, Edessa was noted for the fruitfulness of its soil. One of the main centres of Syrian culture, with its own citadel, Edessa was a prosperous city and a popular resort of merchants.

King Abgar Uchama, who reigned from 13 to 50AD, lived in the capital city of Edessa. The king, however, was dying of a terrible physical disorder. When he heard continual mention of Jesus and his miracles, King Abgar sent a humble request to Him by a letter-carrier named Ananias, begging for relief from his disease.

Eusebius claims to have seen this letter in the archives at Edessa, along with Jesus' reply, and an account of the events that surrounded them. He says he translated them into Greek from the original Syriac. G A Williamson, who translated Eusebius from Greek into English, says that he also had a copy of the Syriac text which states that Jesus gave a verbal message to Ananias who wrote it down.

The account in Eusebius continues :

The letter from Abgar the Toparch to Jesus and sent to Him at Jerusalem by the courier Ananias reads as follows :

"Abgar Uchama the Toparch to Jesus, who has appeared as a gracious saviour in the region of Jerusalem - greeting. I have heard about you and about the cures you perform without drugs or herbs.

If report is true, you make the blind see again and the lame walk about; you cleanse lepers, expel unclean spirits and demons, cure those suffering from chronic and painful diseases, and raise the dead.

When I heard all this about you I concluded that one of two things must be true - either you are God and came down from heaven to do these things, or you are God's Son doing them.

Accordingly I am writing to beg you to come to me, whatever the inconvenience, and cure the disorder from which I suffer.

I may add that I understand the Jews are treating you with contempt and desire to injure you: my city is very small, but highly esteemed, and adequate for both of us."

Jesus' reply to the Toparch Abgar by the courier Ananias :
"Happy are you who believed in me without having seen me.  For it is written of me that those who have seen me will not believe in me and that those who have not seen will believe and live.

As to your request that I should come to you, I must complete all that I was sent to do here, and on completing it must at once be taken up to the One who sent me. When I have been taken up I will send you one of my disciples to cure your disorder and bring life to you and those with you."

In a very short time the promise was fulfilled. After Jesus' resurrection and ascent into heaven, Thomas, one of the twelve apostles, was moved by inspiration to send Jude Thaddaeus to Edessa where he stayed with  a man named Tobias. When his arrival was announced and he had been made conspicuous by the wonders he performed, Abgar was told, "An apostle has come here from Jesus, as He promised you in His letter."

So Abgar sent for him and asked if he was indeed the one whom Jesus had promised.  Jude Thaddaeus agreed he was and said to the king, "You wholeheartedly believed in the One who sent me, and for that reason I was sent to you.  In proportion to your belief shall the prayers of your heart be granted."   Abgar replied, "I believed in Him so strongly that I wanted to take an army and destroy the Jews who crucified Him, if I had not been prevented by the imperial power of Rome from doing so."

Thaddaeus said, "Our Lord has fulfilled the will of His Father and after that He was taken up to the Father."

"I too have believed in Him and in His Father," said Abgar.

"For that reason," replied Thaddaeus, "I lay my hand on you in His name."

When he did this, Abgar was instantly cured of the disease and disorder from which he suffered. Abgar was amazed at this miraculous answer to his prayers. Then others in the assembly came and fell at Thaddaeus' feet to be prayed for and many were likewise miraculously healed.

King Abgar said, "It is by the power of God that you, Thaddaeus, do these things, and we ourselves are amazed.  But I have a further request to make : explain to me about the coming of Jesus and how it happened and about His power."

Thaddaeus replied, "For the time being I shall say nothing; but as I was sent to preach the word, be good enough to assemble all your citizens tomorrow and I will preach to them and sow in them the word of life.

"About the coming of Jesus and how it happened, about his mission and the purpose for which His Father sent Him, about His power and His deeds and the mysteries He spoke in the world.

How He humbled himself and put aside and made light of His divinity, was crucified and descended into Hades, and rent asunder the partition which had never been rent since time began and raised the dead, how he descended alone but ascended with a great multitude to His Father and is now seated on the right hand of God the Father with glory in the heavens, and how He will come again with power to judge the living and the dead."

So Abgar instructed his citizens to assemble at daybreak and hear the preaching of Thaddaeus.

After that the king ordered gold and silver to be given to him. But Thaddaeus refused them  and asked, "If we have left our own property behind, how can we accept other people's?"

Eusebius adds that Thaddaeus exerted such an influence over the people of Edessa that he led them to reverence the power of Christ and made disciples of them.

"From that day to this," (ie around 325AD) writes Eusebius, "the whole city of Edessa has been devoted to the name of Christ, providing most convincing proof of our Saviour's goodness to them also."

Corroborating this is the fact that a list of bishops drawn up by Irenaeus, bishop of Lyons, in 185AD, includes those of Edessa and

Melitene to the north. Also at the church Council of 197AD, held to decide the dating of Easter, there was important input from the bishops of Osrhoene. Then in 205AD, King Abgar the Great made Osrhoene the first kingdom to declare Christianity its state religion.

A sizeable body of Christian literature in the Syriac language was produced at Edessa in the ensuing years,  including a Syriac version of the New Testament and the Acts of Judas Thomas. Then in the fourth century AD The School of Edessa, a Syrian theological school,  was established there.

Eusebius ends his account by quoting the note at the bottom of the Syriac document, "All this happened in the year 340".  Translator G A Williamson states in his footnote, that this was "of the Seleucid era and corresponded to the year AD30, the probable year of the Ascension."

 As Eusebius places this story before the stoning of Stephen, and around the time  James the brother of Jesus was appointed  head of the Jerusalem church, a date of AD30 seems quite probable.

If this is so, it makes Jude Thaddaeus the first of the apostles to obey our Lord's command to take the message of the gospel to those outside of Palestine, and also to  bear witness before  a Gentile king.

Although some have relegated this story to the realm of legend, Williamson says that with Edessa so close to both Jerusalem and Antioch, compared with places like Ephesus and Rome, it would be surprising if the gospel had not been taken there early in the history of the church.

Add to this the fact that the adjoining country of Armenia was evangelised soon after and the Abgar story seems more than credible.

**ARMENIA**

After spending almost five years in Edessa, Jude Thaddaeus is claimed by the Armenian[4] church as being the first of five apostles, along with Mari of the seventy, to have preached the gospel in their country.

In the history of the Armenian church 'Jerusalem and the Armenians' by Assadour Antreassian, on page 20 the author states : "Thus all Christian Churches accept the tradition that Christianity was preached in Armenia by the Apostles Thaddeus and Bartholomew in the first half of the first century.

"The generally accepted chronology gives a period of eight years to the mission of St Thaddeus (35-43AD) and sixteen years to that of St Bartholomew (44-60AD), both of whom suffered martyrdom in Armenia."

Aziz S Atiya in his History of Eastern Christianity writes that the Armenian church claims Jude Thaddaeus as its first patriarch. Armenian bishops are  named as his successors.

The Armenian Church claims that the church founded by Jude Thaddaeus and Bartholomew converted a greater part of the people during the second and third centuries. Then in 301AD, through the efforts of St Gregory the Illuminator, the King of Armenia, Tiridates the Great, and all the members of his family and the nobility were converted and baptized. Following this the king officially declared Armenia to be a Christian country.

## BABYLON

In  Book 6 of  The Apostolic History of Abdias, we are told that Jude Thaddaeus was joined by Simon the Zealot in Babylon.[5]

Although both Isaiah and Jeremiah had prophesied the utter destruction of Babylon some hundreds of years earlier, only part of Nebuchadnezzar's grand city had fallen into disrepair at this stage.

Conquered by Alexander the Great in 333BC, Babylon was then the second city in the empire, after Susa. It was deserted as the seat of power, however, when Alexander's successors, the Selucidae, built their new capital of Selucia on the Tigris, about forty-eight kilometers north of Babylon, in 312BC.

In 171BC the Parthians conquered most of what had been the old Persian empire, including, Babylon, which remained under their rule until 226AD.

The Sassanian Dynasty was next, followed by the Moslem Arabs in 641AD. After this the once great city of Babylon quickly fell into total decay. It  was soon covered by the sands of the desert, and as the prophets foretold, it became the haunt of  wild beasts.

At the time of the apostles, however, Josephus states that the greatest concentration of Jews outside of Jerusalem lived in and around Babylon. Edersheim adds, "it was just between the Euphrates and the Tigris that the largest and wealthiest settlements of the Jews were. Nehardaa, on the Nahar Malka, or royal canal, which passed from the Euphrates to the Tigris, was the oldest Jewish settlement. It boasted a synagogue said to have been built by King Jechoniah with stones that had been brought from the Temple.

In this fortified city, the vast contributions intended for the Temple were deposited by the Eastern Jews and thence conveyed to their destination under escort of thousands of armed men."

He continues, "Only a minority of Jews consisting in all of about 50,000 returned to Jerusalem under Zerubbabel and Ezra. According to Josephus,... vast numbers, estimated at millions, inhabited the Trans-Euphratic provinces."

The great Pharisaic teacher, Hillel, originally came from Babylon. He and his fellow rabbi Shammai lived and taught in Jerusalem in the time of Herod the Great.

Hillel may have presided over the meeting of the Sanhedrin which pointed the Magi to Bethlehem as the birthplace of the Messiah. His disciple, Gamaliel, mentioned in the book of Acts, was the wise and gracious teacher under whom Paul received his rabbinical training.

It was to this still relatively prosperous city of Babylon that Jude Thaddaeus and Simon the Zealot came in 44AD. Here, we are told in the Apostolic History of Abdias, the two apostles preached the gospel and baptised many over a period of fifteen months.

## PERSIA

Then, after ordaining Abdias as Bishop of Babylon, Jude Thaddaeus and Simon, accompanied by many disciples, set out probably in the spring of 46AD, to spend the next thirteen years taking the message of Christ to the twelve provinces of Persia, then under Parthian rule.

During this time they saw large numbers won to the Lord, and witnessed many miracles. They were also able to strengthen the many believers who had been converted to Christ under the ministry of Thomas some twelve years earlier

Their deeds are said to have been recorded by Craton, one of their disciples. They were then included by Abdias in his account of the lives of the twelve apostles which he wrote in Aramaic. Eutropius, Abdias' disciple translated the History into Greek and this was later translated into Latin by Julius Africanus (170-245AD). Although the stories of their exploits seem to have grown with the retelling, the basic details are probably true.

Jude and Simon are finally said to have reached the city of Suanir where they lodged with a chief citizen named Sennes. Their preaching was strongly opposed by the local priests who claimed they were enemies of the local gods. The priests and some of the people are said to have attacked and killed the two apostles on the 1st July, probably of the year 59AD.

This account is often cited as being the occasion of Jude and Simon's martyrdom. However, the considerable details of their individual ministries over the next few years would seem to indicate that if they were indeed attacked at Suanir, they apparently both escaped and lived to serve the Lord elsewhere.

## ARMENIA AND DEATH

If this is so, it would seem that Jude and Simon then made their way to Lesser Armenia where they joined Andrew in early August of 59AD. Here the three apostles apparently served the Lord together until Bartholomew arrived the following spring.

From Armenia, Andrew then moved on to Asia Minor and Simon to Jerusalem and ultimately Britain.

The Armenian church account states that in 60AD[6] Jude Thaddaeus was joined by Bartholomew and that the two laboured together in Greater Armenia for six years.

Then, on the 28th October 66AD, Jude Thaddaeus, now around seventy years of age, is said to have been crucified and then shot with arrows until he died. According to Armenian martyrology, one thousand others, including men and women of noble descent died with Jude Thaddaeus at that time near Mt Ararat.

The original tomb of Jude Thaddaeus is said to be in a small village called Kara Kelisa near the Caspian Sea, about sixty-four kilometers from Tabriz in Iran near the Soviet border. In later years, however, the apostle's bones were removed from here and placed in a special tomb in St Peter's Basilica in Rome.

Whatever we decide about the King Abgar story, or the details of Jude Thaddaeus' sojourn in Persia, there is a considerable body of evidence pointing to Jude Thaddaeus being the first of the apostles to take the gospel to Armenia and to have laboured and ultimately laid down his life in that country.

An Aramaic writing by Jude Thaddaeus was still being used at St Petersburg as late as the eighth century.

Thus another apostle who receives very little notice in the New Testament apparently did quite a remarkable work for God over a period of almost thirty-six years, preparing him for the great responsibilities to be entrusted to him in Christ's future kingdom.

## REFERENCES FOR JUDE THADDAEUS

1. Matthew 10:18, Mark 13:9, Luke 21:12-13
2. McBirnie pp 195-196, Barclay p 117, Mark 3:18,
3. Matthew 10:3, Luke 6:16, Acts 1:13, John 14:22
4. Eusebius (W) pp 65-70, 230, Thiele (L) pp13-15, Barclay pp 118-122, RD Atlas p 205, Halley pp 466, 748, McBirnie pp 203-205, Latourette p 87, History of the World p 255, Enc Brit Vol III p 788, Stoker p 8
5. McBirnie pp 198-200, 204, 231, 133, 136, Barclay p 121
6. McBirnie p 198, 206, Fausset pp 69, 562, 563, Unger (Dict) p 118, Isaiah13:17-22, Jeremiah 51:37-43, Josephus, Antiquities 15:2, Edersheim (M) pp 7-9, 128, Edersheim (S) p 9
7. James pp 464-466, Latourette p 103
8. McBirnie pp198, 200, 203, G Taylor p 53, Latourette p 105

# SIMON THE ZEALOT

While Andrew and Jude Thaddaeus were taking the message of Christ to the people north and east of Jerusalem, Simon the Zealot found his allotted course was to take him west, along the coast of North Africa and as far off as the little known land of Britain.

In the Gospel of the Twelve Apostles[1], mentioned by Origen, Simon is said to have received his call to discipleship along with Peter, Andrew, James, John, Jude Thaddaeus and Judas Iscariot at the Sea of Tiberias.

Simon had apparently been an active member of the Zealots[2] until he decided to follow Jesus, and was designated Simon the Zealot in the New Testament to differentiate between him and Simon Peter.

## ZEALOTS

Josephus tells us that the Zealots constituted the fourth philosophical school in Israel after the Pharisees, Sadducees and Essenes. While the other
three groups were primarily religious, the Zealots were more of a nationalistic party who sought to overthrow the Romans through active resistance and guerilla warfare.

Their aim was to restore the rulership of their nation to their Jewish leaders, under the oversight of God Himself. The Zealots based their actions on the words of Matthias, father of the Maccabees. As he lay dying, Matthias said, "And now, my children, be zealous for the Law, and give your lives for the covenant of your fathers."

In 4BC a large band of Zealots, under the leadership of Judas, son of Hezekiah, sacked the great city of Sepphoris about four miles north of Nazareth. Then, in 6AD Judas the Galilean objected to the Jews having to pay tribute to Rome. He is referred to by Gamaliel in Acts, where he is said to have led a large band of Zealots in an uprising against Rome. In each case their efforts met with death.

In 46AD two sons of Judas of Galilee, Jacob and Simon, were crucified by the procurator, Tiberius Julius Alexander for their rebel activities.

Then in 65AD Gessius Florus took over as procurator of Judaea. From the start he openly antagonised the Jews.

The final straw came when Florus raided the temple treasury and appropriated seventeen talents from temple funds for his own use. He claimed the money was for imperial service, but to the Jews it was sacrilegious and led to a massive riot.

In response Florus crucified several of the leading citizens of Jerusalem and handed over part of the city to his troops to plunder. The Zealots reacted by massacring the entire Roman garrison stationed at the Antonia fortress in early September 66AD. Rome responded with force, leading ultimately to the utter destruction of Jerusalem in 70AD.

The final stand of the Zealots was at Masada in 73AD when they annihilated all nine hundred and sixty of their inhabitants rather than yield to Roman rule.

This, then is the party with whom Simon was primarily aligned. There were within the Zealots, however, two distinct groups. First there were the idealists who preferred to accomplish their goals with a minimum of bloodshed.Then there were those who seemed to relish the idea of guerilla warfare and all that it entailed. In later years many of the latter group became known as sicari, or assassins, from the small curved sica or dagger they carried concealed in their clothing.

Simon was apparently an idealistic revolutionary. Yet Jesus' teaching on loving your enemies and turning the other cheek would certainly have been difficult to reconcile with his aims as a Zealot.

Eventually, however, under the influence of Jesus' love and wisdom, Simon seems to have forsaken his former allegiance to follow the better way, as he thought, of achieving his goals.

Three other men mentioned in the New Testament, however are thought to have been aligned with the assassin group within the Zealot party.

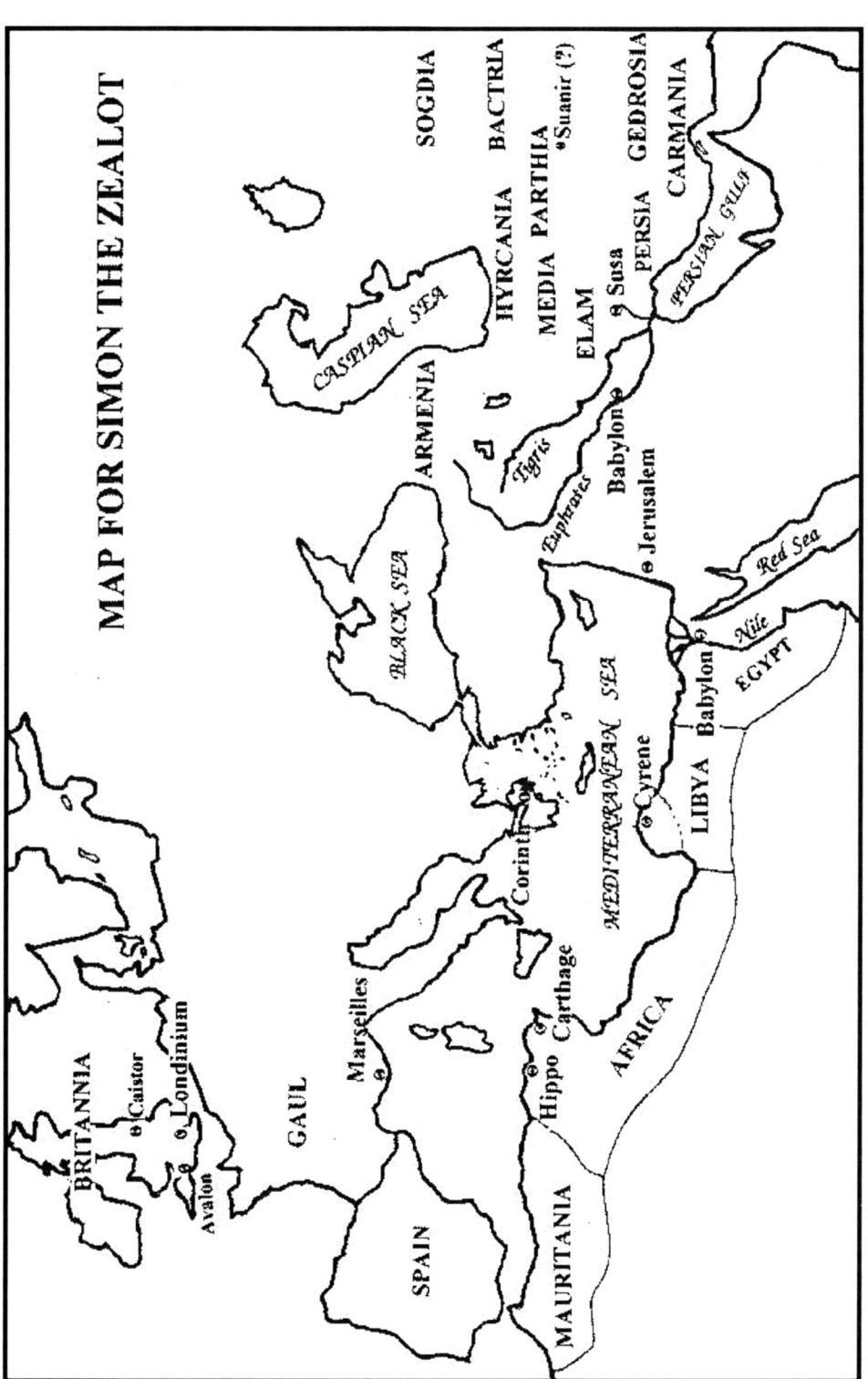

MAP FOR SIMON THE ZEALOT

SOGDIA

BACTRIA

*Suanir (?)

GEDROSIA

HYRCANIA

MEDIA PARTHIA

CARMANIA

PERSIA

ELAM

⊕ Susa

PERSIAN GULF

CASPIAN SEA

ARMENIA

Tigris

Babylon ⊕

Euphrates

⊕ Jerusalem

BLACK SEA

Red Sea

Nile

MEDITERRANEAN SEA

Babylon ⊕

EGYPT

Corinth

⊕ Cyrene

LIBYA

Marseilles
⊕

Carthage
⊕

AFRICA

Hippo ⊕

GAUL

BRITANNIA

⊕ Caistor

⊕ Londinium

Avalon

MAURITANIA

SPAIN

## BARABBAS AND THIEVES

In the gospels we are told that Barabbas,[3] a 'notable prisoner' whose life was exchanged for that of Jesus, was a robber, who had committed murder in an insurrection in Jerusalem. The term used to describe Barabbas is 'archilestes' or bandit chief.

The words 'lestes' or 'lestai', used in the gospels to describe the two thieves who were crucified with Jesus indicate not ordinary robbers but insurgents or rebels. Josephus uses the word 'lestai' in his writings when referring to the Zealots.

The Acts of Pilate tells us that these two were involved with Barabbas in the insurrection. They originally escaped to Jericho. But seven days before Passover they were arrested and brought to Jerusalem where they were tried and condemned, along with Barabbas, to die by crucifixion.

The thief crucified on Jesus' left was named Gestas. We are told that he used to strip and murder wayfarers and was an altogether violent man who knew not God nor obeyed any law.

Dysmas, the one on the right, however, was a Galilean who kept an inn. He despoiled the rich, the account tells us, but did good to the poor, even burying them if necessary.

Dysmas seems to have known about Jesus and his miracles and ministry back in Galilee. He may even have heard Jesus preaching about the heavenly kingdom.

When Jesus prayed on the cross, "Father, forgive them for they do not know what they are doing," Dysmas realised that this was no ordinary man. As his companion taunted Jesus, Dysmas rebuked him saying, "Don't you fear God ... we are getting what our deeds deserve, but this man has done nothing wrong." Then turning to Jesus he said, "Jesus, remember me when you come into your kingdom."

Knowing the man's heart, Jesus promised him, "I tell you the truth, today you will be with me in Paradise."

On the strength of those words the early church enrolled Dysmas as the first person saved through the death of Christ.

After the feeding of the five thousand when the people wanted to make Jesus their king, it is thought they could have been stirred up by the Zealots in their midst. Simon may have been disappointed that day at Jesus' refusal to take the crown offered Him, but he was apparently prepared to await Jesus' timing.

The cross therefore must have cruelly dashed all his hopes and it took the events surrounding the resurrection to partially restore them. It is thought Simon may have been the one who asked Jesus, just before His ascension, if he was now going to restore the kingdom to Israel. This would seem to indicate that even at this late date Simon's eyes were still focussed on an earthly, rather than an eternal kingdom.

All this apparently changed for Simon and the others, however, when they were filled with the Holy Spirit on the Day of Pentecost. Jesus had promised that the Holy Spirit would lead them into all truth, and at last their eyes were opened to understand the truth of the message Jesus had been patiently trying to teach them for the past three years. That His kingdom was not of this world, but was an eternal kingdom to be established in the hearts of individuals who would accept Him as their Saviour and Lord.

When Simon discovered that he had been appointed to take the life-changing message of Christ to the people of North Africa, and even as far away as Britain, he set about it with a zeal that was now inspired by the love of Christ and empowered by the Holy Spirit.

## NORTH AFRICA

There is a considerable body of information regarding Simon's North African[4] ministry, although much of it is fairly brief.

Dorotheus, Bishop of Tyre in the reigns of Diocletian and Constantine, around 303 AD wrote, "Simon Zelotes traversed all Mauritania and the regions of the Africans preaching Christ."

Nicephorus, Patriarch of Constantinople and Byzantine historian (AD 758-829) states, "Simon ... travelled through Egypt and Africa, then through Mauritania and all Libya preaching the gospel."

Dorman Newman, writing in 1685, states "Simon Zelotes is said to have diverted his journey towards Egypt, Cyrene, Africa, Martania and Libya."

The Coptic Church of Egypt affirms that Simon "went to Egypt, Africa and Britain."

Otto Hophan in his book, The Apostles, says : "A third general opinion, which later Greek commentators in particular followed placed the scenes of Simon's Apostolic labours in NW Africa, Mauretania and even Britain." (p285).

The Popular and Critical Bible Encyclopaedia (p 1590) states,

"These traditions assigned a different destiny to Simon, alleging that he preached the gospel through North Africa, from Egypt to Mauritania, and that he even proceeded to the remote isles of Britain."

Before leaving Jerusalem Simon would almost certainly have talked with Mary regarding the route she and Joseph took as they fled from Herod more than thirty years earlier.

With this information Simon would have followed the caravan route down through Gaza and Raphia, then across into the Land of Goshen in north-eastern Egypt. Here the family of Joseph in the Old Testament had settled long ago.

There were many small Jewish settlements in this area and Simon would have eagerly shared the message of the Messiah with each group he met. Some may even have recalled the little family who stayed briefly with them on their journey south.

The present-day Coptic church readily points out the places, including a large cave, a well and sycamore tree, where the Holy Family[5] is said to have rested along the way.

The bole of this sycamore tree is claimed to still exist in the balsam gardens of Mataria, about nine kilometers north of Cairo on the right bank of the Nile. The Queen of Sheba is said to have brought seeds of the fragrant balsam tree as a gift to Solomon and a special garden of these waist-high trees was planted near Jericho.

When Cleopatra received Jericho and its surrounds as a gift from Mark Antony, she took cuttings of these balsam trees, along with Jewish gardeners to tend them, and set up the famous gardens at Mataria, near Heliopolis, site of the ancient city of On. An obelisk erected in Abraham's time is still standing there to this day.

After moving on from here, it is claimed Mary and Joseph finally settled in the Jewish quarter of the Roman fortress of Egyptian Babylon just south of the future city of Cairo. The crypt of the church of Abu Sargah is said to mark the site of the house in which they stayed.

Simon apparently spent some time preaching in this Egyptian Babylon and it is claimed the town has been inhabited by Christians ever since the first century.

From Babylon, Simon no doubt travelled extensively down the length of the Nile, preaching primarily to Jewish settlements situated in the towns along its banks. Eventually, with the weather cool enough to travel, Simon set off, probably in the company of a trader's large camel caravan, to share the good news of Christ with the towns along the coast of North Africa.

Each city had its own strong Jewish quarter which sought to uphold its Hebrew faith in the midst of Greek culture and Roman militarism. One of the most important of these was the leading Libyan city of Cyrene.

## CYRENE

On the Day of Pentecost, among those who heard the apostles speaking the wonderful works of God in their own language were men from "Egypt and the parts of Libya near Cyrene[6]."

Founded by a family of Dorians around 630BC, Cyrene rapidly became a flourishing commercial centre. Captured by Alexander the Great in 331BC, the area around Cyrene was quickly colonised by the Greeks, with four other cities soon established in what became known as Cyrenaica. In 322BC the province came under the rule of Ptolemy I of Egypt who named it the Pentapolis, in recognition of its five major cities.

Cyrene, the capital, was built on a large fertile plateau a hundred and twenty-eight kilometers wide. Standing 2000 ft above sea level, the land then sloped downward in a series of terraces to the bustling port city of Apollonia, thirteen kilometers to the south-west. Richly fertile soil, adequate rainfall and an agreeable climate made the entire area, and Cyrene in particular, like one huge oasis in an otherwise barren, sandy wasteland that constituted 90% of the land of Libya.

In 96BC Ptolemy Apion, in his will, left Cyrenaica to the Romans who later established it as a Roman province.

By the time Simon arrived, Cyrene was a prosperous city of more than 100,000 people, enjoying a lifestyle that included Greek culture, wealthy Phoenician traders, Roman military oversight, and for the Jews, freedom to worship Jehovah as they chose.

The Cyrenian Jews had an established synagogue in Jerusalem. Its members were among those who disputed with Stephen and eventually had him stoned.

There were others from Cyrene, however, who had witnessed the miracle of Pentecost. They had repented of their sins, received

Christ as their Saviour, been filled with the Holy Spirit and were among the initial three thousand baptised by Peter and the other apostles.

These new believers had returned home, probably with a copy of the Sayings of Jesus prepared by Matthew[7], and had spread the good news of the Saviour among their townsfolk.

One of these was most likely Simon[8] of Cyrene, the man pressed by the Romans into carrying the cross of Jesus. When Mark wrote his gospel for the Christians in Rome he referred to Simon as "The father of Alexander and Rufus", indicating that the two sons were apparently well known to the Roman church.

Simon the Zealot seems to have spent some years at Cyrene, preaching the message of salvation through Christ, healing the sick and building up the new believers into a strong church.

In Acts we are told that in the dispersion of the Christians after the stoning of Stephen, some went as far as Antioch, preaching to the Jews only. These were followed by men from Cyprus and Cyrene who preached to the Greeks there as well.

Then at the prayer meeting held in Antioch around 44 AD, when Paul and Barnabas were commissioned for missionary service, among the prophets and teachers present were Simon called Niger and Lucius of Cyrene.

Simon the Zealot's teaching and influence could well have prepared these men for their own missionary outreach.

In later years the church at Cyrene became a great Christian centre from which the gospel went forth all over North Africa and even to other countries.

## CARTHAGE

From Cyrene Simon would have travelled along the famous Sirte Route. This coastal road ran for four hundred and forty kilometers from Misratah to Benghazi, skirting the Gulf of Sirte just a short distance in from the Mediterranean Sea. The extended highway ran from Alexandria to Carthage[9]. Along the way Simon would have preached in well known towns like Leptis Magna, Oea (modern Tripoli) and Sabrata before finally reaching Carthage.

Founded as a large trading post by the Phoenicians of Tyre around the time of Jereboam of Israel, Carthage soon developed into one of the great cities of antiquity. However in 146 BC the Romans completely destroyed Carthage, even spreading salt over its remains.

Then in 29BC Caesar Augustus built a new city on the site, naming it Colonia Julia Carthago - or Carthage. Augustus centred the administration of the Roman provinces of Africa there and the city grew rapidly. By 20AD it was said to equal Alexandria in both size and culture.

Simon seems to have spent several years establishing and building up the church in this prosperous city. He apparently laid the foundations well, as by 177AD Carthage was considered to be one of the leading centres of Christianity, along with Antioch, Ephesus and Alexandria. From its ranks came great Christian leaders such as Tertullian and Cyprian.

## HIPPO

Simon's next main stop would have been at the somewhat smaller town of Hippo[10] near the modern town of Bone in Algeria. A community with partial rights of Roman citizenship, the town was settled by people from Carthage around 400 BC. Apparently a strong church was established here also, and from 395-430AD the famous Christian writer Augustine was its bishop.

Numerous authors tell us that Simon then preached the gospel "all over the Roman province of Mauritania", establishing churches as he went.

Some indication of the wide spread of Christianity throughout the whole of North Africa is shown by the fact that at the Council of Carthage in 216AD there were no less than seventy-one African bishops.

In 45AD, some twelve years after Simon's visit, Mark is said to have preached in his home town of Cyrene. Atiya states that he then took a copy of his gospel to Alexandria and subsequently established a strong church there.

Bartholomew, James the Less and Matthew are also mentioned as having preached in Egypt. However, no other apostle, apart from Simon, is credited with having preached the gospel throughout the whole of North Africa.

It would appear that Simon's former zeal for his nation had indeed been transformed into a burning zeal to spread the message of his Saviour's love to all he met.

## BRITAIN

Simon's work was not finished yet, however. Nicephorus, after outlining Simon's ministry in North Africa adds, "And the same doctrine he taught to the Occidental Sea and the Isles called Britanniae[11]."

Dorman Newman, following his details on Africa continues, "Nor could the coldness of the climate benumb his zeal or hinder him from shipping himself over into the Western Islands, yea even to Britain itself."

Fox's Book of Martyrs states, "Simon, surnamed Zelotes, preached the gospel in Mauritania, Africa and even in Britain, in which latter country he was crucified."

Rather than joining himself to Joseph of Arimathea's group at Avalon in the west of Britain, Simon apparently arrived by ship at the port of London and remained there for his first brief sojourn on British soil.

The Romans claimed to have founded the city of London after defeating the local inhabitants in 43AD. However, British annals state that London was founded by a Trojan named Brutus back in 1020BC, two hundred and seventy years before the founding of Rome. He named the city Troia Nova or New Troy, which eventually came to be known as Trinovantum.

Lud, the elder brother of Cassibelaunus, surrounded the city with lofty walls and towers built with extraordinary skill and changed its name to Kaerlud, or Lud's city. When he died Lud was buried near the gateway now known as Ludgate.

In time the city became known as Kaerlundein, then Londinium, and eventually, London. The city covered about one hundred and forty hectares along the north bank of the Thames. From as early as 1000BC the British had carried on a brisk trade with Phoenician and Greek traders at this well known port.

In 54BC, after failing to conquer the British in two campaigns, Julius Caesar signed a treaty with the British pendragon, Cassibelaunus, at Verulam. Caesar and his men then moved on to Londinium where the British entertained the Romans magnificently from the 10th to the 26th September.

In 43AD the Romans conquered the area around Londinium. They erected their garrison along the northern bank of the Thames.

It stretched from the temple of Diana, the present site of St Paul's, to the white mount, where the white tower of the Tower of London now stands.

This then, is the London at which Simon disembarked. According to Hippolytus and Cardinal Baronius, Simon's first arrival in Britain was in 44AD at the height of the Claudian war.

With the upheaval of war all around him, it was virtually impossible for Simon to preach openly for long, and it seems he soon boarded a ship for home.

Sixteen years were to elapse before Simon returned to fulfil his appointed ministry in the land of Britain.

## PERSIA

When Simon arrived back in Jerusalem he seems to have caught up with his old friend, Jude Thaddaeus. After no doubt reporting on their travels to the home church, the two then apparently set out for Babylon.[12]

Here, the Apostolic History of Abdias tells us, they spent a fruitful fifteen months, winning many for the Lord, healing the sick and baptising the new believers. Then, after ordaining Abdias as bishop of Babylon, along with deacons and other helpers, they set off to take the gospel further afield.

Simon and Jude Thaddaeus are said to have spent the next thirteen years travelling throughout the twelve provinces of Persia, now under Parthian rule, winning many new converts and strengthening the believers.

After almost losing their lives at Suanir, Simon and Jude Thaddaeus eventually reached Armenia around early August of 59AD. Here they joined Andrew in preaching the gospel and establishing the Christians.

Simon is claimed by the Armenian[13] church as one of five apostles to have planted the message of Christ in their land. Early in 60AD Simon returned to Jerusalem were he joined up with a group who were preparing to leave for Britain.

## BRITAIN

George Jowett writes, "In the year 60AD special mention is made of Joseph (of Arimathea) going to Gaul and returning to Britain[14] with another band of recruits, among whom is particularly mentioned Simon Zelotes, one of the original twelve. This was the second journey to Britain for Simon Zelotes and his last."

Dorman Newman's account continues, "Here (in Britain) he is said to have preached and wrought many miracles and after infinite troubles and difficulties which he underwent, suffered martyrdom for the faith of Christ, being crucified by the infidels and buried among them."

Dorotheus writes, "He was at length crucified, slain and buried in Britain."

The Genealogies of the Saints in Britain, quoting Dorotheus, names Aristobulus as the first of our Lord's disciples to be martyred in Britain, (in 59AD), with Simon Zelotes being the second, nearly two years later.

George Jowett goes on, "Simon was unusually bold and fearless. He decided to conduct his evangelising campaign in the eastern part of the island which was more heavily populated with Romans. It was far beyond the protective shield of the Silurian arms... In this dangerous territory Simon was definitely on his own."

Simon spent almost a year preaching in and around London and over the south-eastern part of Britain.

Jowett goes on, "Undeterred, with infinite courage, Simon began preaching the Christian gospel right in the heart of the Roman domain. His fiery sermons brought him speedily to the attention of Catus Decianus, (the officer whose atrocities were the immediate cause of the Boadicean war). But not before he had sown the seed of Christ in the hearts of Britons and many Romans."

Tacitus states that more than 80,000 Romans and British civilians perished under Boadicea, around 40,000 of them in London itself, which gives some indication of the size of the city at that time.

## DEATH

"Simon was finally arrested, under the orders of Catus Decianus, the Roman praefect at Caistor", continues Jowett. "As usual his trial was a mockery. He was condemned to death and was crucified by the Romans at Caistor, Lincolnshire, and there buried circa May 10th, AD 61.

"The day of the martyrdom of Simon Zelotes is officially

celebrated by both the eastern and western church on May 10th and is so recorded in the Greek Menology (record of Martyrs).

Cardinal Baronius, in his Annals Ecclesiastici, gives the same date in describing the martyrdom and burial of Simon Zelotes in Britain."

Thus Simon, the former Zealot, attained a martyr's crown after serving his Lord with unflagging zeal for over thirty years. Yet he had the joy and fulfilment of helping to usher in a far greater Kingdom than the one he had envisaged that day back in Judea so many years before.

## REFERENCES FOR SIMON THE ZEALOT

1.  McBirnie p 207
2.  Matthew 10:4, Mark 3:18, Luke 6:15, Acts 1:13, Josephus : Antiquities 9:9, 18:4-25, 20:252-258, BJ ii, 293-332, 1 Maccabees 2:50, Acts 5:37, FF Bruce (NT Hist) pp 80-95, 320-360, McBirnie p 220, Barclay pp 90-94
3.  Matthew 27:15-26, Mark 15:7, Luke 23:18-19, 32-33,39-43, John 18:40, FF Bruce (NT Hist) pp 92-95,194, Fausset p 683, John 6:1-15, Acts 1:6, James pp 103-104, 161-163, Edersheim (M) Vol II pp 597-601
4.  McBirnie pp 208-212, Lewis p 117, Morgan pp 127-128, Jowett pp 157-159, Jerome p 364
5.  Halley p 419, Fedden pp 96-97, Keller pp 337-339
6.  Acts 2:8-10,37-41, Edersheim (M) Vol I, p 62, Young's Concordance p 218
7.  Eusebius(W) p 152
8.  Matthew 27:32, Mark 15:21, Acts 11:20, 13:1, Halley p 570
9.  McBirnie pp 209-210, Halley p 764, Enc Britannica Vol II, p 598
10. Halley p 764, Enc Britannica Vol V, p 55
11. McBirnie p 207, Fox (Z) p 5, Jowett pp 36, 153-154, Lewis pp 20, 26, Morgan pp 75,110, 127-128, 137,148, Monmouth pp 73-74,106-107
12. McBirnie pp 231, James pp 464-466
13. McBirnie p 207
14. McBirnie p 207, Fox (Z) p 5, Forbes p 92, Morgan pp 137, 142, Jowett pp 154, 157-159, 188, Lewis p 117

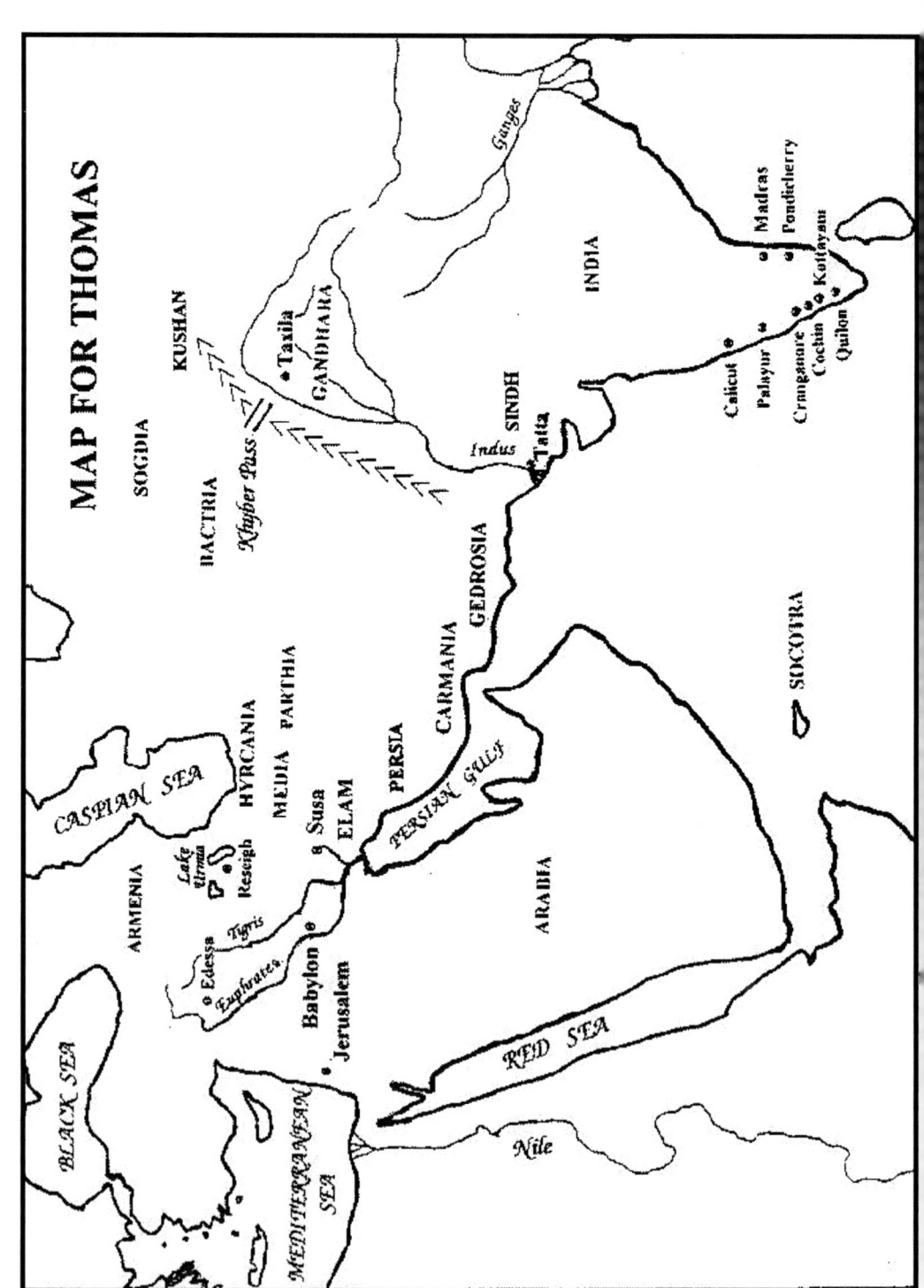

# MAP FOR THOMAS

# THOMAS

The apostle Thomas,[1] has carried the stigma down through the years of being a classic doubter. Yet there was much more to Thomas than his reluctance to accept that Jesus really had risen from the dead.

His name appears more than half-way down the lists of the apostles, usually before or after Matthew. Both the Hebrew name Thomas and its Greek equivalent Didymus, mentioned three times by John, mean twin. Later writings refer to the apostle as Judas Thomas, or Judas the Twin, but in the New Testament he is just referred to as Thomas, or Thomas the Twin.

Whether Thomas's twin brother or sister was still living we don't know, but as there is no mention of Thomas seeking to bring his twin to Jesus, it would seem likely that he or she was no longer with him.

If the usual inter-dependence of twins had been broken, this could account in part for Thomas's tendency to melancholia. A sense that something was missing from his life causing a deep loneliness within. As though he was always searching for something just out of reach.

Then Jesus came into Thomas's life, and His love and acceptance more than filled the void left by Thomas's absent twin. So much so that Thomas gave Jesus his unwavering loyalty and devotion, even being willing to die with Him if necessary.

Thomas's selection as one of the Twelve is recorded in the first three gospels and Acts, but John is the only writer who gives us any further details regarding this apostle. From this it has been concluded that Thomas was a native of Galilee, a fisherman and no doubt a friend of John.

John tells us that after the Jews had sought to stone Jesus, He withdrew with his disciples to Perea on the far side of Jordan, two days' journey from Jerusalem. When news reached them that Lazarus was dying, Jesus waited two more days then said, "Let us go back to Judea." The other disciples sought to dissuade Jesus from returning to imminent danger, but Thomas said to them, "Let us also go, that we may die with Him."

After the Last Supper when Jesus was telling his disciples of the heavenly home He was going to prepare for them He added, "You know the way." Thomas said, "Lord, we don't know where you are going, so how can we know the way?"

This led Jesus to give his memorable reply, "I am the way and the truth and the life. No-one comes to the Father except through me."

When Jesus was finally arrested, tried and crucified, Thomas's whole world shattered around him. In his overwhelming despair and loss, Thomas the loner couldn't even share his grief with the other disciples. Blindly he stumbled from the scene of the crucifixion most likely up into the rocky mountains behind Jerusalem. Here he remained for some time, possibly in one of the many caves, where he no doubt wept in utter despondency and brokenness.

When Thomas eventually made his way back to the other disciples he was greeted with the amazing news that Jesus had risen from the dead and had appeared to them all. But Thomas's grief had been too deep to allow himself to be carried away by what he felt were just the hallucinations of grieving men. Patiently he tried to explain to them that when people long deeply enough for something they can convince themselves that it has really happened when it hasn't.

He concluded with the impassioned words, "Unless I see the nail marks in his hands and put my finger where the nails were, and put my hand into his side, I will not believe it."

A week after His first appearance to his disciples, Jesus again stood among them and said, "Peace be with you!". Then turning to Thomas, He said, "Put your finger here, see my hands. Reach out your hand and put it into my side. Stop doubting and believe."

Thomas said to Him, "My Lord and my God!" Then Jesus told him, "Because you have seen me, you have believed: blessed are those who have not seen and yet have believed."

In spite of his initial doubts, however, Thomas was the first person recorded as confessing that Jesus was both Lord and God.

The last mention we have of Thomas is when he and six other disciples went fishing on the Lake of Galilee while they waited for

Jesus to again appear to them. The following morning Thomas was one of those treated to a special breakfast on the beach prepared by the Lord himself.

After his inclusion in the list of those praying in the upper room, there is no further mention of Thomas in the New Testament. Yet as McBirnie points out, "We really know more about St Thomas than we do about almost any other apostle with the exception of John and Peter."

## WORLD DIVIDED

When the apostles divided the world between them, Eusebius, Socrates, Latourette and others tells us that Thomas was given Parthia.[2] At that time the kingdom of Parthia stretched from the Tigris to the Indus and from the Persian Gulf to the Caspian Sea.

The Acts of Thomas states that the apostle was given India. Yet a large part of the narrative of the Acts also describes Thomas's ministry in Parthia.

However, it relates that the night Thomas was assigned India, he told the Lord, "I am a Hebrew man; how can I go amongst the Indians and preach the truth?" Then the Saviour appeared to him and said, "Fear not, Thomas, go to India and preach the word there, for my grace is with you."

From numerous accounts we find that Thomas travelled all over Parthia preaching the gospel for almost twenty years, including several spent at Taxila in north-west India near the River Indus. Then in July of 52AD it is claimed that Thomas arrived at Malabar in South India. Here he witnessed fearlessly for his Lord for about seven years, before crowning his service in martyrdom at Mylapore, a suburb of Madras on the eastern coast.

## BABYLON

Thomas's first main area of service after leaving Jerusalem was Babylon.[3] One of the largest centres of Jewish learning outside of Jerusalem, Babylon was home to many direct descendants of those carried into captivity by Nebuchadnezzar in Daniel's time.

The Church of the East claims that it was 'founded by the apostles, St Peter, St Thomas, St Thaddaeus and St Mari of the Seventy'.

Mar Yacob Manna, a Uniate Bishop of the Roman church writes,

"Places where Patriarchates were organised by the holy apostles are the following mothers of all cities, the first, Babylon... then Alexandria, Antioch, Rome and Constantinople."

Rev Enoch Jones of the American Episcopal Church writes, "The Patriarchate of the East can claim to be the oldest Patriarchate."

## WISE MEN

Among those who heard Thomas preach in Babylon were apparently the Wise Men[4] or Magi who had visited the baby Jesus many years before.

A Souvenir of India, states, "The Church of the East traces its origin directly back to the original apostles. One of its chapels founded by the Three Wise Men on their return from Bethlehem, is still in use today in the town of Resaieh, in Northern Iran. The (present) Patriarch attended that chapel as a boy."

Dorman Newman, writing in 1685, says, "In Persia he (Thomas) met with the Wise Men whom he baptised and took along with him."

The Magi, or Wise Men who visited the baby Jesus, are considered to have been learned astrologers/astronomers from the university city of Sippar, forty-eight kilometers north-west of Babylon.

One of the greatest observatories of the ancient world was situated at Sippar, enabling astronomers to read and interpret the stars with great accuracy for their times.

Built by Nimrod, Sippar was one of the places where Hammurabi's laws were set up. It is also the city where, tradition says, the Sacred Writings were buried before the Flood and afterward dug up.

In its vast libraries were the writings of Daniel, one of its earlier Chief Magi, in which the coming of the Messiah was foretold. Another scroll contained the prophecy of Balaam regarding a Star arising in Jacob. From these and other writings the Wise Men are thought to have interpreted a new star in the heavens as heralding the birth of a special and important Messiah-King in Israel.

If the above accounts are correct, it would seem that the Wise Men heard Thomas preaching in Babylon, responded to the message they had been waiting more than thirty years to hear and were baptised by the apostle. They then added their testimony to that of Thomas as he preached throughout the country. They may even have taken him to the town of Reseigh on the west bank of Lake Urmia and shown him the chapel they had built so many years before.

The Souvenir of India states, "The holy apostle St Thomas, after establishing the first Christian church among his own people in ancient Babylon, turned to India, led by the Holy Spirit, and with an evangelical zeal traversed this subcontinent preaching the good news and baptising those who believed in Him."

McBirnie writes, "It is evident that Thomas visited Babylon. Because the tradition of the western churches revolved around Constantinople and Rome, it is astonishing how little is known, even by many church historians, about the many other vital Christian movements which began during Apostolic times.

"These movements quickly spread *eastward*, and therefore owed nothing to western Christianity. But the traditions are clear, there was an Apostolic movement eastward and Thomas was a central figure."

## PARTHIA

On the day of Pentecost, among those who heard the apostles extolling the wonderful works of God in their own languages were Parthians,[5] Medes, Elamites, and residents of Mesopotamia.

Sophronius, in his additions to Jerome's Lives of Illustrious Men, says Thomas preached the gospel "to the Parthians, Medes, Persians, Carmanians, Hyrcanians, Bactrians and Magians and died at Calamina in India."

Dorman Newman continues his account, "The Apostolical assigned to St Thomas was Parthia.Afterwards he preached the gospel to the Medes, Persians, Carmans, Horcany, Bactria and neighbouring nations."

Fox backs up the range of Thomas's ministry throughout Parthia. He writes, "Thomas preached to the Parthians, Medes, Persians, Carmanians, Hyrcanians, Bactrians and Magians. He was killed in Calamina, India."

One of the provinces, rich with Jewish history, that Thomas no doubt visited after Babylon was Elam. Named after a son of Shem, the Elamites gave their name to the region east of the River Tigris, south-west of Media and north of Persia proper.

Susa the capital, on the banks of the River Karka, was three hundred and twenty kilometers east of Babylon. From here the

Persian Royal Road had, from ancient times, stretched all the way to Sardis in Anatolia.

At Susa (or Shushan) Queen Esther and Mordecai played out their life and death struggle with the wicked Haman. Here, too, Nehemiah waited on King Artaxerxes, and Daniel apparently spent some time at Susa, as his tomb is shown just south of the city.

Travelling south Thomas would have passed through Persia before reaching Carmania on the southern coast. He may have pushed on into the arid, inhospitable regions of Gedrosia that skirted the Arabian Sea before retracing his steps.

From Persia he probably made his way through Elam into Media, and thence to Hyrcania on the southern coast of the Caspian Sea.

Thomas and those who followed him must have planted the seed well, as by 225AD more than twenty bishoprics existed in the Tigris-Euphrates Valley and on the borders of Persia. They stretched from near the Caspian Sea to the Bahrein Islands in the Persian Gulf.

Continuing on through Parthia proper, Thomas faithfully preached the gospel in Sogdia and Bactria before reaching the Khyber mountain range which separated Bactria from India.

While Thomas was preaching in Bactria, possibly at Alexandria or one of the other large towns founded by Alexander the Great three hundred years previously, one of his converts was apparently a Syrian trade envoy from Edessa named Haban (or Abbanes) in the employ of the Parthian King Gondophares of Gandhara.

## TAXILA

Most of the evidence for the next period of Thomas's life and ministry is derived from the apocryphal Acts of Judas-Thomas. This rather fanciful document is believed to have been written by the famous Edessene writer Bardesanes (154-222) towards the end of the second century.

It is said to be based on reports of Thomas's ministry related by his assistant Haban, when he brought the apostle's bones back to Edessa following his martyrdom in India.

The Acts of Judas Thomas had generally been dismissed as fables. Then in the 19th century archaeologists digging in the Gandhara region, uncovered a large stone inscription along with numerous coins containing the names of both Gondophares and his brother

Gad, showing that Gondophares had ruled over the area from 19AD to at least 45AD.

King Gondophares ruled from his capital city Taxila,[6] a 'wealthy, prosperous, well-governed and fortified city, laid out on a symmetrical plan and of a comparable size to Ninevah' according to ancient writers.

Situated between the Indus and Jhelum rivers, Taxila was at the junction of three major trade routes.

Its university, where more than sixty arts and sciences were taught, was famous from at least the 7th century BC and attracted scholars from all parts of India. The prophet Buddha studied there in the 6th century BC.

A satrapy under the Persian king Darius I in the 5th century BC, the city fell to Alexander the Great in 326BC. By the time Thomas arrived the city was under Parthian rule.

The Encyclopaedia Britannica states: "According to early Christian legend, Taxila was visited by the apostle Thomas during the Parthian period."

After crossing the Khyber mountains with Haban at the famous Khyber Pass, Thomas soon found himself entering this impressive city which had become a melting pot of Indian, Iranian and Greek culture. Greek and Aramaic were both widely spoken in Taxila and the surrounding province of Gandhara enabling Thomas to communicate readily throughout the whole area.

Although the Acts of Judas Thomas gives us many fanciful details regarding Thomas's time there, other accounts seem to back up the fact that Thomas did indeed spend the next four or five years working in and around Taxila, preaching the gospel, healing the sick and leading many to the Lord, including King Gondophares and his brother Gad.

Some accounts claim that Thomas even went as far as Tibet, just across the border from the Punjab in the northern Indus Valley during this time.

## TATTA

Then around 50AD, word came that the aggressive Kushans were sweeping down from the north with the kingdom of Gandhara in their sights. King Gondophares must have persuaded Thomas and

Haban to escape and the two fled down the Indus River to the town of Tatta[7] situated near its mouth.

They apparently spent some months there preaching the gospel. Thomas may even  have left a copy of Matthew's gospel with his new converts at Tatta.

Atiya and others relate that there are still Christians at Tatta today who claim to be descended from those first converts of Thomas.

A protestant mission report from Sindh states that there are some fakirs (ascetics) with their headquarters at Tatta who profess themselves as followers of Thomas the Saint. They practise a number of Christian rites and possess a book which they call the Gospel of St Matthew.

## SOCOTRA

The Romans had been trading with India for many years and had established trading posts along the east and west coasts of southern India.  They sailed from Red Sea ports during July and August using the mid-summer monsoon winds.  Then in December and January they made the return trip laden with spices, pepper, spikenard, cotton, muslin, sandalwood, ivory and  precious stones.  Some even sailed as far as China to bring back coveted silk products and rare gemstones.

Because of the prevailing winds, during December Thomas could only obtain passage from Tatta to the island of Socotra[8] off the south-east coast of Arabia.

A small island of around three thousand square kilometers, Socotra had long been famous for its flora, including myrrh, frankincense and the dragon's blood tree.

The population was a mixture of native Arabs and  Indians as well as the Greeks who had been settled on the island by Ptolemaeus. These people welcomed Thomas warmly and a strong church was established there, with most of the island's inhabitants eventually embracing Christianity.

In the fourteenth century Marco Polo wrote, "The inhabitants of this island  are baptised Christians, but their archbishop has nothing to do with the Pope in Rome, but depends upon the archbishop of Baghdad." Socotra maintained a strong Christian witness until the 17th century.

## MALABAR

With the arrival of the Monsoons early in July, Thomas embarked once more for India.

The church of South India claims that Thomas landed at Cranganore on the Malabar[9] Coast in July of 52AD, and each year they celebrate the anniversary of his landing.

In 1964 the Indian government produced a stamp with a picture of St Thomas, commemorating his arrival on the Malabar coast in July 52AD.

There was a large population of Jews, Syrians and Greeks all along the four hundred kilometers long  by eighty kilometers wide Malabar Coast. Thomas was therefore able to preach in either Aramaic or Greek, with some of the local Dravidian population also understanding Greek.

According to the Acts of Judas Thomas, the apostle "ceased not preaching to them that this is Jesus Christ whom the scriptures proclaimed, ... who was crucified and raised the third day from the dead.   And the fame of him went forth into all the cities and countries and all that had sick or them that were oppressed by unclean spirits brought them and some they laid in the way whereby he should pass, and he healed them all by the power of the Lord."

During his almost seven-year ministry in this area, Thomas is said to have converted high caste Hindu families in Cranganore, Palayur, Cochin, Quilon and other towns, consecrated church leaders from some of these families, built seven churches and led a great many of the common people to the Lord.

According to a stone inscription and several other accounts, it is claimed that Thomas converted three emperors and six kings in all of India.

Many other writers back up the concept of Thomas's ministry in both Parthia and India.

The Roman Breviary states that Thomas "handed over the precepts of the Christian Faith and life to the Parthians, the Hyrcanians and the Bactrians, and taking himself to the Indians, instructed them in the Christian religion."

St Gregory Nazienzene (AD 330-389) wrote, "And the apostles, were they not foreigners ... Andrew in Epirius, John in Ephesus and Thomas in India?"

St Ambrose who died AD 397 wrote, "Even kingdoms shut in by rugged mountains were accessible to them, as India to Thomas ..."

Venerable Bede states, "Peter received for share Rome, Andrew Achaia, James Spain and Thomas India."

## MADRAS

According to the Acts of Judas Thomas, the apostle "was proclaiming the word of God throughout all India", when a captain of King Mazdai of Madras[10] arrived. He pleaded with Thomas to come over to the eastern coast of India and pray for his wife and daughter who had been demon possessed ever since a brutal attack on them three years earlier.

Thomas was greatly grieved for them, and said to the captain, whose name was Siphor, "Do you believe that Jesus will heal them?"

When the captain said he did, Thomas then led him to pray and commit himself to Christ.

After this Thomas called the Christians together and ordained Xenophon the deacon to watch over them. Then, taking his leave of the brethren Thomas, apparently accompanied by Haban, went with captain Siphor to Mylapore.

Here he prayed for the man's wife and daughter and their recovery was so miraculous that they and the captain became dedicated Christians. The Acts states then that 'many assembled from every quarter to see the apostle of the new God'.

Thomas fearlessly preached the gospel to them and over the ensuing months he had the joy of seeing a large number come to know the Lord.

Around this time, some accounts say that Thomas embarked on a Roman trading ship to China and preached there for several months until the return voyage of the ship.

On Thomas' return to Madras, the wife of the king's brother was converted. This so infuriated her husband that he asked his brother to arrest Thomas as a sorcerer.

The king sent his wife to try and reason with his brother's wife, but she was so affected by her sister-in-law's changed life that she accompanied her to the captain's house where Thomas was again staying.

When she, too, became converted, the king had Thomas arrested and thrown into prison.    But the king's son accompanied his mother and aunt to the prison to hear Thomas preach, and he too became a Christian. The son's  wife, who had an incurable illness, was also healed by Thomas' prayers.

## MARTYRDOM

The king was so furious that he had Thomas brought to court, where, with the support of the local Brahmin priests, he had him pronounced guilty of sorcery. The king, however, was concerned about the reaction of the people. So he instructed his soldiers to take Thomas to a mountain just outside the town and spear him to death. Thomas asked the soldiers for permission to pray first, then, still kneeling, he told them to do what they had to. He was struck with four spears and died[11] within a short time.

Thomas was mourned by multitudes of people and the king's son erected a magnificent tomb on the spot where the apostle was killed. That mountain is called Mount St Thomas to this day and is situated in the town of Mylapore, a suburb of Madras. A stone cross erected on the site gives the date of Thomas' death as the 21st December in the 30th year of the promulgation of the gospel', or 60AD.[10]

The Syntaxarum of the Church of Constantinople has the following, "Thomas preached the word of God to the Parthians, the Medes, the Persians and the Indians, and was pierced with lances by these latter."

Buchanan, a pioneer Protestant missionary, writes, "We have as good testimony that Apostle Thomas died in India as that Apostle Peter died in Rome."

Some time later, the king's youngest son was dying, and the king decided to see whether the bones of Thomas would heal his son. When he opened the tomb he found the body had gone.

So the king took some dirt from the tomb and laid it on his son and prayed to the God of Thomas to heal him.   He did and the king and all his family finally became Christians and joined the church pastored by his former captain, Siphor, who had first brought Thomas to Mylapore.

## EDESSA

But what had happened to the body of Thomas. The Nestorian

church and other accounts claim that after the apostle's martyrdom, his assistant, Haban took his bones back to Edessa[11] where another tomb was built for them. Socrates and Sozomen both mention a magnificent memorial church in Edessa built to commemorate Thomas and his martyrdom in India. In later years missionaries were sent from Edessa and other parts of Parthia to minister to the St Thomas Christians in India.

In 295 AD the Chronicle of Seert refers to Bishop David leaving his See of Basrah to devote himself to a missionary life in India.

At the Council of Nicea in 325 AD one of the signatories was 'John of Persia, Bishop of all Persia and of Great India'.

However, Persian monks who went to oversee the churches in South India were not always welcome. Some were told by the local bishops, "We are the disciples of St Thomas; we have nothing to do with the See of Mari."

In 345 AD the monk Theosophilus was sent by Constantius to India where he reformed several 'abuses', including that of sitting during public readings of the gospel.

When Roman Catholic missionaries arrived in India in the 16th century, they reported that the St Thomas Christians only had a cross at the summit of their churches with no bell and no engravings or graven images, as St Thomas had prohibited them.

More than fifteen hundred years after Thomas' ministry in India, it seems the people were remaining true to the teachings of their own apostle.

Atiya states that there are nearly a million present-day Christians in the South-India districts where Thomas laboured. Because of their industry, ability and integrity they are highly regarded by all castes and are considered just below the Brahmins. The Hindus often seek cures from their ailments by bringing gifts to the Christians when seeking their prayers.

So we find that Thomas, the erstwhile doubter, became Thomas the faithful and loyal apostle. For more than thirty years after the resurrection he earnestly and whole-heartedly proclaimed the gospel Jesus had given his life for and saw it confirmed by miraculous healings. We can imagine Thomas' great joy as he finally stood humbly before his Lord to receive his Master's commendation and a well-earned martyr's crown.

# REFERENCES FOR THOMAS

1. Matthew 10:2-4, Mark 3:16-19, Luke 6:12-16, Acts 1:13, John 10:31, 40, 11: 1-16, 14:1-6, 20:24-29, 21:1-12, McBirnie p 144
2. Eusebius(W) p 107, Latourette p 101, James p 365, Barclay p 49 (Soc 1:19)
3. McBirnie pp 144,146, Jackson p 4, Latourette pp 21, 103
4. McBirnie pp 145, 169, Fausset p 444, Halley p 48, (Sippar), Daniel 2:44,48, 4:9, 5:11, 9:25, Numbers 24:17 (Balaam)
5. Acts 2:5-11, McBirnie p 169, Fox (B) p 5, Barclay p 49 (Soph), Jackson p 42, Latourette p 103
6. Enc Brit Macro Vol IX pp 356, 848, Micro Vol 17 p 1082-1083, Micro Vol 5 p 952, DeSouza p 5, 7, 8, 20, Tisserant p 5, McBirnie pp 149, 167, James pp 371, 375-376
7. Atiya p 363, McBirnie p 149, DeSouza p 23
8. Enc Brit, Macro Vol IX p317, 355, DeSouza p 10, Tisserant pp 4-6, 11-12 Latourette p 100, McBirnie p 149, Atiya p 360
9. Atiya pp 172, 361, DeSouza pp 13-19, Tisserant pp 4, 6, 23,
10. McBirnie pp 147-150, 153, 159, Henry & Scott p 552, James p 392
11. Atiya p 261, McBirnie p 159, James pp 393-395 NIV p 1565, Fox (Z) p 4, (B) p 5, DeSouza pp 13-19, McBirnie pp 153, 160 168, 170, James pp 410-411, 425, 434-438
12. Barclay pp 49-50 (Soc 4:18, Soz 6:18), DeSouza p 14, Atiya pp 245, 359-376, Tisserant p 4, McBirnie pp 149, 165

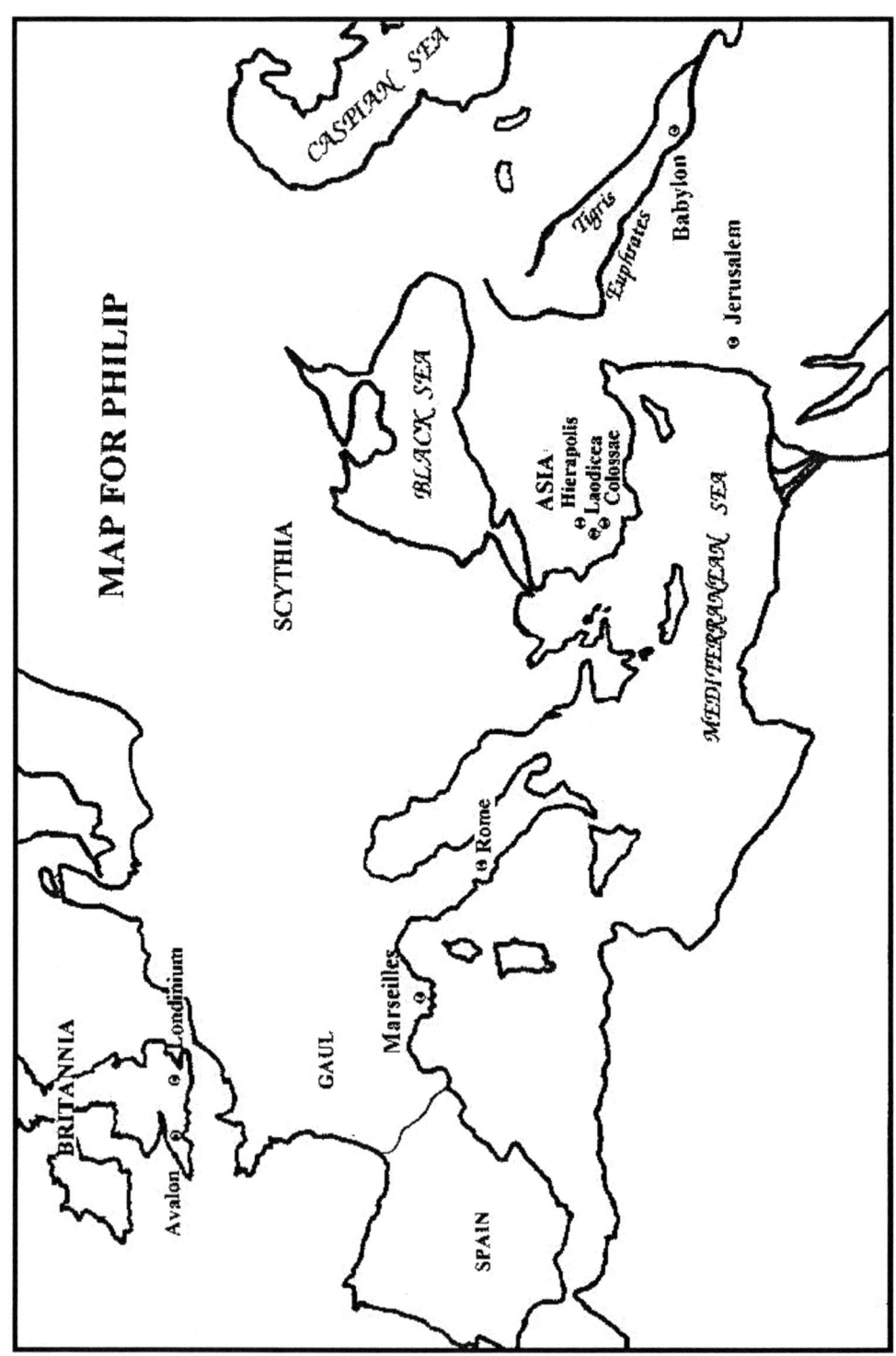

MAP FOR PHILIP

# PHILLIP

Philip, practical and level-headed, was the first of the apostles to receive the call, "Follow Me!" from the lips of Jesus.[1]  Immediately he sought out his more studious friend, Nathaniel Bartholomew, and brought him to Jesus. Confronted by Jesus'supernatural knowledge, Nathaniel readily acknowledged Him as the long-awaited messiah, and joined Philip in becoming one of Christ's most ardent disciples.

Although the two friends don't figure prominently in the gospel accounts, yet in their later ministries, both spent themselves tirelessly in dedicated service for their Lord. Finally the two friends almost sealed their testimony in martyrdom together.

Some confusion has occurred, however, over the fact that two Philips are mentioned in the Book of Acts. The first is Philip the apostle, who is listed among the twelve in the first three gospels and Acts.[2]   The second is Philip the Deacon.[3]

## PHILIP THE DEACON

When the Hellenists or Greek-speaking Jews in the early church felt their widows were not receiving as much practical help as the local Jewish widows, the apostles told them to choose seven men, apparently all Greek-speaking Jews, to oversee the matter.

After Stephen, leader of the seven, was stoned, the others fled Jerusalem during the persecution that ensued. Among them was Philip, Stephen's fellow deacon, who went down to Samaria and preached Christ to the people with amazing results. The church at Jerusalem sent Peter and John to investigate and they prayed for the new converts to be filled with the Holy Spirit.

Soon after this the Lord directed Philip to a desert road where he led an Ethiopian eunuch to faith in Christ. After baptising him in water, Luke tells us the Spirit of the Lord caught away Philip and the eunuch saw him no more. Philip, however, appeared at Azotus, and preached the gospel in all the coastal towns until he reached Caesarea. This may have been Philip's original home town as the Roman Martyrology states that Philip the deacon-evangelist lived and died in Caesarea.

When Paul was on his final trip back to Jerusalem some twenty-six years later, he and his companions stayed at the home of 'Philip the evangelist, one of the seven'. He states that Philip had four unmarried daughters who prophesied. As Philip the apostle also had either three or four daughters who assisted him in the Lord's work, this has added even more to the confusion over the two men.

## PHILIP THE APOSTLE

Philip[4] was a native of Bethsaida, the original home town of Peter and Andrew. He is said to have been of the tribe of Zebulon. John, in his gospel, tells us all we know about Philip other than his name. This would seem to indicate that the two were close friends before they followed Jesus and that Philip was probably a fisherman like most of the other disciples.

At the feeding of the five thousand, Jesus asked Philip, "Where may we buy bread that these may eat?" Philip answered, "Two hundred denarii (or a year's wages) would not buy enough bread for them all to get even a little piece."

It has been suggested from this that Philip may have been in charge of feeding arrangements for the twelve, and that he had already been calculating what it would take to feed the multitude. This would seem to imply a certain astuteness, if not faith, on Philip's part.

Philip is a Greek name and Greek influence was far stronger in Galilee than it was in Judea. The third time we catch up with Philip is just a few days before the crucifixion. Jesus had been preaching in the temple when a group of Greeks came to Philip and asked if they could see Jesus. Philip went and told Andrew and together they took the men to Jesus.

This led Jesus to speak of His imminent death and He asked God to glorify His name. A voice from heaven responded, "I have glorified it and will glorify it again." The people around Him were amazed, including, apparently, the Greeks.

Jesus then uttered His memorable words, "But I, when I am

lifted up from the earth, will draw all men to myself," indicating the manner in which He was to die.

A few days later when Jesus and His apostles were gathered in the upper room following the Last Supper, Jesus again told them that He was going to the Father.   Philip was puzzled, and said, "Lord, show us the Father and that will be enough for us."   Jesus turned to him and said, "Don't you know me Philip even after I have been among you such a long time?  Anyone who has seen me has seen the Father."

Philip is included in the list of those gathered in the upper room on the Day of Pentecost, and wherever Luke mentions 'the apostles' in the early days of the church, Philip would undoubtedly have been one of them. Yet after this there is no further mention of him in the New Testament.

There are quite a number of references to Philip, however, along with his wife and daughters, in the writings of the church fathers and later historians which give us a fairly reliable account of his overall ministry.

Clement of Alexandria[5] wrote that both Peter and Philip  had families, and that Philip gave his daughters in marriage. He also mentions that the wives of the two apostles travelled with them in their missionary work and "helped them in ministering to women at their homes, and by them the doctrine of the Lord penetrated, without scandal, into the privacy of women's apartments."

There is ample evidence in the writings of the early church  that Philip's main sphere of service was at Hierapolis, and that it was here that both he and at least two of his daughters died and were buried.

## PHILIP IN GAUL

There are also other quite strong, although somewhat later traditions, that Philip preached the gospel in Gaul.[6]  These appear to be based on early accounts but the details are not given.

Gaul is not mentioned in the New Testament but when Paul tells Timothy that Crescens has gone to Galatia, a footnote in the RSV says, "Other ancient authorities read Gaul." Philip is the only one of the twelve apostles said to have ministered in Gaul, and  in the accounts of the early Gallic church Philip is referred to as the Apostle of Gaul.

Isidore, Archbishop of Seville, AD 600-636, in his Historia, writes:

"Philip of the city of Bethsaida, whence also came Peter, preached Christ to the Gauls and brought barbarous and neighbouring nations, seated in darkness and close to the swelling ocean to the light of knowledge and port of faith.  Afterwards he was stoned and crucified and died in Hierapolis, a city of Phrygia, and having been buried with his corpse upright along with his daughters, rests there."

British historian, Bede, born about AD 673, assigned Gaul to Philip at the foot of the third tome of his works.

Julian, Archbishop of Toledo, AD 680-690, also states that Philip was assigned to Gaul.

Freculphus, Bishop of Lisieux, France, AD 825-851, wrote : "Philip ... whose daughters were outstanding prophetesses, and of wonderful sanctity, ... as ecclesiastical  history narrates, preached Christ to the Gauls."

Summarising his information regarding Philip, Cardinal Baronius, AD 1596, in his Ecclesiastical Annals wrote, : "Philip, the fifth in order is said to have adorned Upper Asia with the gospel and at length at Hierapolis ... to have undergone martyrdom, which also John Chrysostom hands down, and they say that the same man travelled over part of Scythia, and for some time preached the gospel along with Bartholomew.   In Isidore one reads that Philip even imbued the Gauls with the Christian faith."

Archbishop Ussher, AD 1581-1656, who devised a system of dates for the King James Bible, also asserted, "St Philip preached Christ to the Gauls."

Irenaeus, pupil of Polycarp, became Bishop of Lyons, Gaul, in AD 177, taking over what was apparently a thriving Christian work there.

Tertullian, writing around AD 208, stated,   "The extremities of Spain, the various parts of Gaul, the regions of Britain inaccessible to the Romans are subject to Christ."

Various accounts state that Philip arrived at the port of Marseilles, Gaul, within a few years of the crucifixion and with the dedicated help of his wife and daughters, established a strong church there.

Cardinal Baronius, Freculphus and others then claim that in AD 36 a group of missionaries under the leadership of Joseph of Arimathea landed at Marseilles.

Philip prayed with them and consecrated twelve of their number, including Joseph, Lazarus and his sisters for missionary work in Britain.

## JOSEPH OF ARIMATHEA

Joseph of Arimathea[7] is mentioned in all four gospels.  He was a rich man, with an impressive home in Jerusalem, and a large estate at Arimathea, (present-day Ramalleh), about twelve kilometers north of Jerusalem on the main highway to Nazareth.

The gospels tell us that he was a good and upright man, a prominent member of the Council (Sanhedrin), and had not consented to them crucifying Jesus.  He was also 'waiting for the kingdom of God', or the coming of the Messiah.  John adds that he was a disciple of Jesus, but secretly, because he feared the Jews.

Apparently  the crucifixion caused Joseph to cast aside his fears. We read that he went in boldly to Pilate and requested the body of Jesus, to prevent it being cast into the common grave used for paupers and criminals.It says something for Joseph's standing in the community that Pilate readily gave his  permission, without first checking with the other leaders of the Sanhedrin.

Joseph is said to have owned extensive tin mines in Cornwall and to have made regular trips between there and Jerusalem.    In Jerome's Vulgate version of the New Testament and other sources, Joseph is termed the 'Nobilis Decurio' or 'Minister of Mines' in the Roman government of Palestine.

The Phoenicians traded with Cornwall for its tin from as early as 1000 BC, with the Greeks and Romans later continuing this practice. As the Romans were very dependent on British tin, and later lead from the Mendip mines in Somerset, this could also account for Joseph's high standing with Pilate.

Nicodemus,[8] a leading Pharisee and member of the Sanhedrin, who three years previously had visited  Jesus at John's house at night, was apparently a close friend of Joseph.  He had earlier spoken up in defence of Jesus at a meeting of the Sanhedrin.

The two men carefully wrapped the body of Jesus in linen cloths together with an expensive mixture of myrrh and aloes.  After which they laid it in Joseph's freshly hewn tomb in a nearby garden.

Tradition tells us that Nicodemus was later baptised by Peter, and that he eventually died as a martyr for his faith in Christ.

After Pentecost, we are told, Joseph became the  leader of the Bethany Band, which met in the home of Mary, Martha and Lazarus. Zacchaeus, the former tax collector from Jericho,  was a member of this 'house church', as was Restitutus, the man born blind who had been  healed by Jesus.

## LAZARUS

In a Life of Lazarus,[9] written by the monks of the Abbey at Bethany, we read, "St Lazarus, after the ascension of Jesus Christ, remained for a time in the company of the apostles, with whom he took charge of the church which was at Jerusalem.

"After this he went to the Island of Cyprus in order to escape from the persecution which arose about Stephen. Having filled there for several years the office of a missionary priest, he entered into a ship and traversing the sea, by the grace of God arrived at Marseilles. Here he served God to whom he had entirely consecrated his life, in righteousness and true holiness. He preached the word of Life to those who had not yet received it, and gained many converts to Jesus Christ."

Lazarus is thought to have spent about five years at Citium on the south-east coast of Cyprus where he established a strong church. He is said in a number of accounts to have been its first bishop.

The present church at Citium, near modern-day Lanarca, claims to show visitors the empty tomb of Lazarus to this day.  However, as the church at Marseilles has a similar claim, with his original tomb at Bethany, Lazarus has the odd distinction of having three tombs to his name.

It is thought that his bones may have been taken back to Cyprus some years after his death at Marseilles. That he did in fact minister in both Citium and Marseilles, however, is backed up by a fair amount of evidence.

Epiphanius, Bishop of Salamis, Cyprus from 367AD, tells us that Lazarus was thirty years old when Jesus restored him to life, and that he lived another thirty years afterwards.

## BRITAIN

After staying with Philip at Marseilles for a short time,  Joseph and his eleven companions, including Lazarus, Mary, Martha and their maid, Marcella, set out for Britain[10] where they are said to have settled at Avalon, later called Glastonbury from the glassware made there.

British historian Gildas the Wise, writes that the light of the gospel reached Britain in the last year of the Emperor Tiberias. As Tiberias died on the 16th March 37AD, this would fit with Joseph and his party arriving in Britain late in 36AD.

Archbishop Ussher states : "The British National Church was founded AD 36, one hundred and sixty years before heathen Rome confessed Christianity."

Lazarus, and his sisters, seem to have spent some time in Britain as accounts of his work and some of his teachings are recorded in the British Triads. One of these reads, "The Triad of Lazarus, the three counsels of Lazarus: Believe in God who made thee; Love God who saved thee; Fear God who will judge thee."

However, the ancient church records at Lyons state, "Lazarus returned to Gaul from Britain to Marseilles, taking with him Mary and Martha. He was the first appointed Bishop. He died there seven years later."

Roger de Hovedon, AD 1868, writing of Marseilles, says, "Here are the relics of St Lazarus, brother of Mary and Martha, who held the Bishopric for seven years."

Other accounts mention Lazarus as the first bishop of Marseilles and state that he held this position for seven years. During this time, according to Jowett, he erected a church on the site where the present cathedral now stands. He continues, "His zealous preaching and kindly disposition left a deep impress in Gaul, to such an extent that he is better remembered in France than is Philip, regardless of the latter's long sojourn in Gaul."

The tombs of Lazarus, Mary, Martha, Marcella, Zacchaeus, Restitutus and Maximin, said to have been one of the seventy, are shown in France to this day.

## HIERAPOLIS

After spending some years heading up the work in Gaul, Philip and his family apparently then moved to the Roman city of Hierapolis,[11] in Phrygia, Asia Minor. As Gaul was originally settled by people from Galatia, Philip may have been asked by his Gallic converts to take this wonderful new message back to their relatives in Asia.

Hierapolis is mentioned by Paul in his letter to the Colossians, around 63AD, when Philip was presumably back in Gaul. Speaking of Epaphras, Paul says that he had a great zeal for the people of

Colossae, Laodicea and Hierapolis. These three major cities of the Roman province of Asia were located in the forty kilometer long valley of the Lycus River. Roman highways connected them with Ephesus, one hundred and sixty kilometers to the west, and right through to Antioch and Babylon in the east.

Colossae was situated in the upper part of the Lycus Valley around sixteen kilometers south-east of Laodicea, and just north of the 8,000ft Mt Cadmus.

Laodicea on the banks of the Lycus River, boasted a large medical school whose physicians prepared the famous Phrygian powder used to treat ophthalmia.

In John's letter in the book of Revelation addressed to the luke-warm Christians of this prosperous city, he encourages them to anoint their eyes with eyesalve that they might see spiritual truths more clearly.

Hierapolis, where Philip and his family settled, was situated ten kilometers north of Laodicea and twenty-five kilometers from Colossae on an elevated terrace one hundred and fifty meters above the Lycus plain. The town was famous for its medicinal spa of hot sulphur springs which was visited by sick folk from all over the world.

The original settlers of Hierapolis were Greeks from Macedonia and Pergamum with a mixture of some native Phrygians. There were also numerous Romans and a sizeable Jewish segment. Many gods were worshipped there, including Greek, Roman and Oriental deities, as well as the Jewish Yaweh, or Jehovah.

In 60AD, while Philip was once more absent in Gaul, a severe earthquake levelled much of Hierapolis and Laodicea. Both towns were quickly rebuilt, however, with Hierapolis boasting two theatres, a large gymnasium and impressive Roman baths, with massive stone arches.

A main thoroughfare spanned the town from northwest to southeast with streets crossing at right angles. A basilica on the east side of the main street dating to the second half of the first century AD still bears the Chi Rho monogram and may be dedicated to St Philip, although there are also three other Christian churches dating from early times.

Philip was ideally suited to minister to the mainly Greek-speaking population of this Roman-Greek city. He also had the opportunity of reaching the many visitors to the health spa, who could then take the message of Christ back with them to their home-lands.

One of Philip's daughters is said by Polycrates, Bishop of Ephesus, AD 190, to have married, and lived and died at Ephesus. Clement states that Philip gave his 'daughters' in marriage'. This would seem to imply that there were four daughters. His two unmarried daughters, however, were apparently quite active in helping Philip with the work at Hierapolis and are said to have converted many.

Papias[12] who was born in Hierapolis around 70AD, later became Bishop of Hierapolis, and was martyred in 155 AD. In his "Expositions of the Oracles of the Lord," he tells us that he heard the daughters of the Apostle Philip speaking in Hierapolis.

They related how a dead person, (named by Papias as the wife of Manaen, who grew up with Herod the Tetrarch) was raised from the dead.

They also told how Justus, surnamed Barsabas, whose name was put forward with that of Matthias to fill the place of Judas, swallowed a dangerous poison and by the grace of the Lord was none the worse.

## SCYTHIA

In the Apostolic History of Abdias, Book X, we are told that twenty years after the ascension, around 50AD, Philip set out on an even more dangerous missionary venture, to take the gospel to the barbarous Scythians[13] in the area to the north-west of the Black Sea.

He remained there for one year, during which time many were saved and healed and some were even raised from the dead.

Finally, after baptising several thousand new converts, Philip ordained bishops and other leaders to care for them and returned to his work in Hierapolis.

## STACHYS

In Paul's epistle to the church at Rome, around 57AD, he sends greetings to his 'beloved Stachys'.[14] Some time after this, Stachys, said by Hippolytus and Dorotheus to have been one of the seventy, apparently travelled to Hierapolis to assist Philip in the work there.

The Acts of Philip tells us that Stachys held meetings in his own home, and after Philip's death, he remained in charge of the work at

Hierapolis apparently until the arrival of Andrew the following year. Nicephorus, historian and later bishop of Byzantium, tells us that, soon after this, Stachys was ordained by Andrew as the first bishop of Byzantium.

However, in 60AD, with Stachys presumably caring for the believers at Hierapolis, Jowett states that Philip was back in Gaul consecrating a second group of missionaries bound for Britain. These included Simon the Zealot and Joseph of Arimathea's son, Josephes, whom Philip had baptised.

The third time Philip is mentioned as consecrating a team of missionaries under Joseph's leadership is in 65AD.

## BARTHOLOMEW & MARTYRDOM

In 66AD, Philip returned to Hierapolis where, towards the end of that year, Chrysostom and the Acts of Philip tell us, he was joined by his old friend, Bartholomew.[15]

The two friends ministered together at Hierapolis for almost a year, during which time Nicanor, the wife of the proconsul was healed and became a dedicated Christian. This so infuriated the proconsul that he had Philip and Bartholomew arrested and thrown into prison. At one stage the proconsul is reported to have told Philip, "Denounce Jesus and save your lives." Philip answered, "Accept Jesus and save your soul."

At first both were sentenced to be crucified, but for some reason, at the last minute, Bartholomew was released. Philip,[16] however, was brutally pierced through the ankles and thighs and fastened upside down to a cross, before being stoned to death. According to Nicephorus this happened on the 15th November, probably of 67AD when Philip was around seventy years of age.

Early Christian writers are unanimous that Philip's tomb, along with those of two of his daughters, can be seen at Hierapolis.

However, Pope John the Third (560-572) acquired the body of St Philip from Hierapolis and interred it in a new church in Rome which he named "The Church of the Holy Apostles Philip and James." The bones of the two apostles can still be seen in a large marble sarcophagus under the altar there.

From rather obscure beginnings in the New Testament, Philip the pragmatic disciple, seems to have worked tirelessly and with lasting results for his Lord, in at least two, and possibly three foreign countries.

As Stephen was dying, he caught a glimpse of Jesus standing, waiting to receive him into glory. On the day of Philip's martyrdom, we can imagine the apostle being greeted by Jesus himself with the loving words, "Well done, good and faithful servant. Enter into the joy of your Lord."

## REFERENCES FOR PHILIP

1. John 1:43-51
2. Matthew 10:2-4, Mark 3:16-19, Luke 6:12-19, Acts 1:13
3. Acts 6:5-8, 8:5-40, 21:8-10, Unger (A:NT) p 154, (Dict) p 858
4. John 1:44, 12:21, Fausset p 568, McBirnie p 122, John 6:5-7, 12:20-33, 14:8-10, Acts 1:13
5. Eusebius(W) p 140-141, 151, 231, Fausset p 562, 1 Corinthians 9:5, James p 469
6. Jowett pp 64-65, 157, 205-206, McBirnie pp 125-128, Fausset p 562, Lewis pp 112-114, II Timothy 4:10 (RSV footnote), Latourette p 98
7. Matthew 27:57-60, Mark 15:42-46, Luke 23:50-53, John 19:38-42, Fausset p 398, Taylor p 41, 140-141, Morgan p 117, Lewis pp 56, 100, Dobson p 19, Jowett pp 16-19, Churchill pp 6, 9, 10, Fausset p 573
8. John 3:1-21 7:45-53, Taylor p 41, Papini p 196, McBirnie p 108
9. John 12:9-11, Acts 11:19, Unger (Dict) p 651 (Epiphanius), Morgan pp 122, 124, McBirnie pp 126, 272-279, Jowett pp 163-164, Taylor pp 51, 88-89, 104, 107, 189
10. Taylor p 141 (History of Gildas sections 8,9), Morgan p 116, Eusebius p 77, FF Bruce (NT Hist) p 36, Jowett p 80
11. McBirnie pp 123-124, Unger (A:NT) pp 264, 270-273, Colossians 4:12, Eusebius p 141, James p 469
12. Acts 1:23, 13:1, Eusebius(W) pp 140-141, 150-151, 231
13. McBirnie pp 123-124, 127, James p 469
14. Romans 16:9, Unger (Dict) pp 51-52, 1044, James pp 448-450
15. James pp 448-450, McBirnie p 127, 131, Jowett p 65
16. Eusebius(W) pp 141, 231, McBirnie pp 123, 129, Fox (Z) p 3

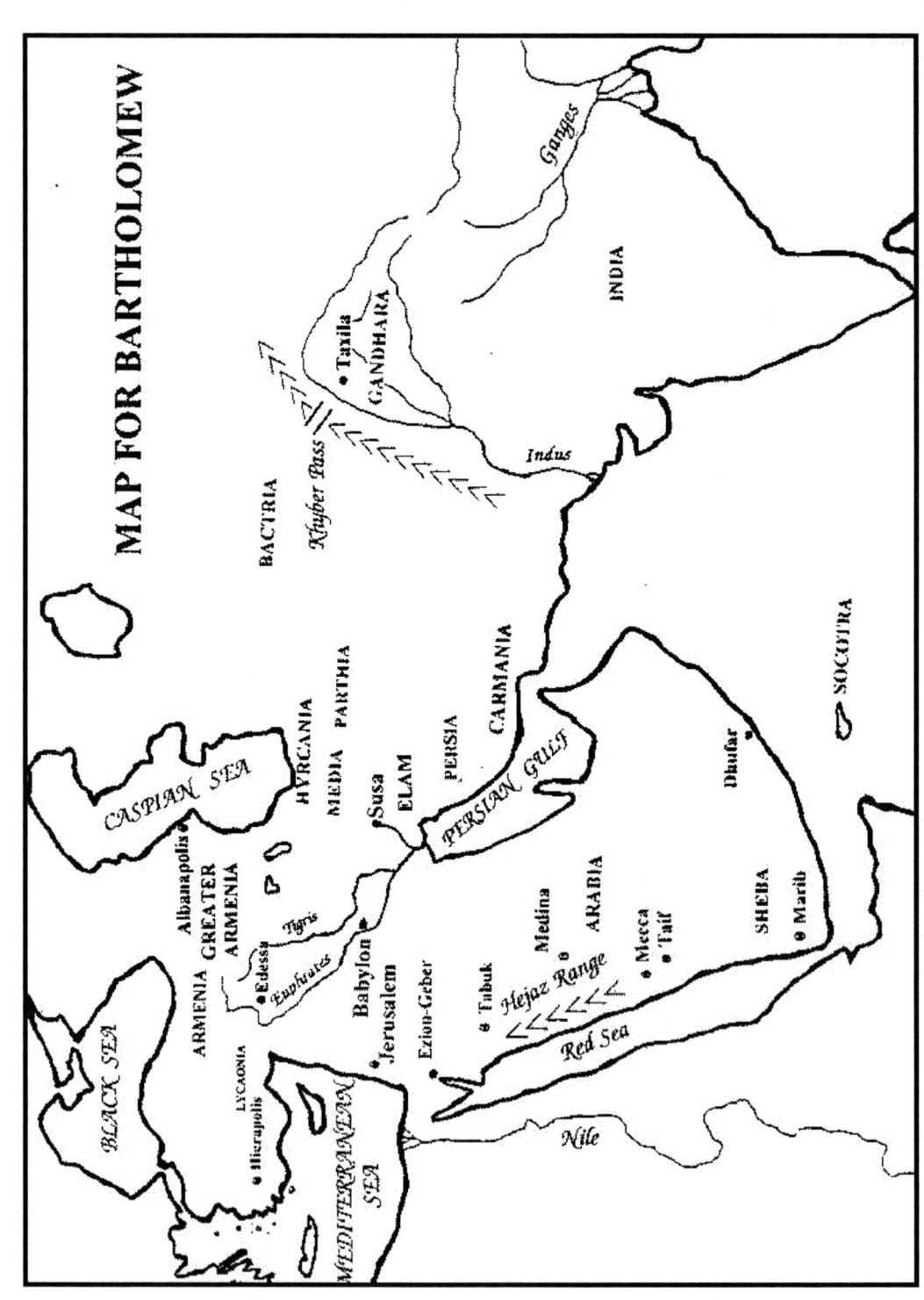

MAP FOR BARTHOLOMEW

# BARTHOLOMEW

When Jesus saw Nathanael Bartholomew approaching, He said to his companions, "Here is a true Israelite, in whom there is nothing false!"[1]

Shortly before Philip called him, it would seem Nathaniel had been praying and meditating under a large, overhanging fig tree. Most ordinary houses in Palestine at that time consisted of one large room. Those wanting a place of solitude to pray often sought it outdoors under their fig tree. These household trees could grow to a height of five meters, with their drooping branches spanning up to eight meters.

When Philip told Nathanael they had found the Messiah, Jesus of Nazareth, Nathanael's immediate response was, "Nazareth! Can any thing good come from there?"

Philip calmly responded, "Come and see."

As they approached the others, Nathanael heard Jesus' comment and asked in surprise, "How do you know me?" Jesus replied, "I saw you while you were still under the fig tree before Philip called you." Amazed, Nathanael declared, "Rabbi, you are the Son of God; you are the King of Israel."

Nathanael had apparently been meditating on the Old Testament story of the angels ascending and descending the ladder in Jacob's dream. Indicating that He knew even Nathanael's thoughts, Jesus said to him, "I tell you the truth, you shall see heaven open and the angels of God ascending and descending on the Son of Man."

In the lists of apostles in the first three gospels Philip and Bartholomew always occur together while in John's gospel Nathanael is obviously a close friend of Philip. Thus, from early on, it has been understood that Nathanael's surname was Bar Tholomew, or Bar Tolmai, meaning 'Son of Tholomew' or Tolmai. Virtually all accounts of Nathanael's later ministry, however, refer to him just as Bartholomew.

According to the Genealogies of the Twelve Apostles, Nathanael was of the house or tribe of Naphtali.

From the list of disciples who decide to go fishing after the resurrection, we learn that Nathanael came from the little village of Cana.    Built on high ground, Cana was approximately eight kilometers north-east of Nazareth, and about twenty-four kilometers south-west of Capernaum.

After his meeting with Nathanael, Jesus returned to Galilee with his six new disciples (presuming John had brought his brother James to Jesus by then), to attend a wedding held in Nathanael's home town of Cana.   Here the disciples witnessed what John states was Jesus' first miracle, that of turning the water into wine.   John adds that after witnessing this miracle, Jesus' disciples put their faith in him.

Approximately a year later, after a wide-ranging ministry in both Judea and Samaria, Jesus returned to Cana with his disciples.   Here, John tells us, Jesus  performed his second miracle in Galilee.

The son of a nobleman was sick in Capernaum.  Learning  that Jesus was in Cana, the father immediately set out  to plead with Jesus to heal the lad.  Jesus assured the man his son would live.   When the nobleman arrived home the following day, his servants reported that the boy had recovered at the very time Jesus had said he would.

Witnessing these two miracles in his home town must have had quite an impact on Nathanael Bartholomew.

Although we don't hear any more of him in the New Testament after the Day of Pentecost, there is quite a bit of information regarding Bartholomew's later ministry both in the Apocryphal Acts and in various church histories and other sources.

His three main areas of service are generally accepted as being Arabia, India and Armenia, where he eventually met  martyrdom.

While there is considerable information regarding Bartholomew's years in Armenia, scholars are divided as to whether the India mentioned in the Gospel of Bartholomew and by other early writers was actually the Indian sub-continent or just Arabia Felix.  However, various strands of evidence would seem to point to him having ministered in both places.

Iranian church leaders state, "By commonly accepted tradition the honour of sowing the first seeds of Christianity in Armenia, and of watering them with their blood, rests with St Thaddaeus and St Bartholomew, who are consequently revered as the First Illuminators of Armenia.

"St Bartholomew's labours and martyrdom in Armenia are generally acknowledged by all Christian Churches. It is said that after preaching in Arabia, the South of Persia and the borders of India, he proceeded to Armenia where he suffered martyrdom by being flayed alive and then crucified, head downward, at Albac or Albanopolis, near Bashkale."

Although we only have dates for Bartholomew's time in Armenia, by linking him up with other apostles, we can arrive at a possible outline for his overall ministry beginning with his early years in Arabia.

The Apostolic History of Abdias[2] describes Bartholomew as being of middle height, with black curly hair covering his ears, white skin, large eyes, straight nose, his beard long and bristling. He wore a white robe with a purple stripe and a white cloak. He prayed often, was always cheerful and spoke many languages.

## ARABIA

Among those who heard the disciples praising God in their own language on the Day of Pentecost were people from Arabia.[3]

When the apostles divided the nations between them, Bartholomew is said to have been allotted Arabia.

Many Jews, particularly those released from captivity in Babylon, had settled in the coastal towns and along the prosperous trade routes of Arabia over the centuries. Most of these would have spoken Aramaic, although trade was generally transacted in Greek. Bartholomew could therefore have preached to his fellow countrymen in their own language, while the native Arab population would have understood Greek well enough to respond to his message.

From Jerusalem, Bartholomew would have followed the road which led down past Jericho. Crossing the Jordan at Bethany, where John had baptised Jesus a few years earlier, he would have soon reached the King's Highway. This ancient road ran north to Damascus, where trade routes from Tyre in the west met up with those leading east to Palmyra, Babylon and ultimately India and China.

Turning south on this well worn highway, Bartholomew would have passed through Heshbon of the Old Testament, skirted Herod's fortress at Machaerus, crossed the river Arnon and pressed on past the Nabatean capital of Petra.

After a long, hot trek of almost three hundred and twenty kilometers, the apostle would have arrived at the port of Ezion-Geber, at the head of the Gulf of Aquaba on the Red Sea. From this ancient port, Solomon's navy sailed as far as China in its search for exotic goods. Bartholomew apparently spent some time in this strategic town of palm groves and copper mines, sharing the gospel primarily with Jews and other 'God-fearers'.

From there he no doubt set off along the ancient Incense Route down the western coast of Arabia. The Queen of Sheba would have travelled this road when she made the nearly two thousand kilometer journey from her capital of Marib in Sheba, to visit King Solomon in Jerusalem almost one thousand years earlier.

Frankincense used in the temple worship at Jerusalem came from the Boswellia trees of Dhufar on the southern coast of Arabia. Myrrh, the main ingredient of the holy anointing oil, was distilled from the resin of the small, thorny Commiphora trees. These grew in the cooler mountain areas of the wealthy kingdom of Sheba in the Yemen section of South-west Arabia, and on the nearby island of Socotra.

The gifts of frankincense and myrrh presented to the baby Jesus by the Wise Men and the myrrh provided by Nicodemus to embalm the Lord's body probably also came from this area.

Rome had invaded the coastal Hejaz region and Yemen in 24BC, renaming the area Arabia Felix.

In the Preaching of St Bartholomew in the Oasis, mentioned by Budge, the apostle is referred to as preaching in the oasis of Al Bahnasa.

East of the Hejaz Range from Tabuk in the north to the cooler, rose and fruit-growing town of Taif, south of Mecca, lay a series of date-palm growing oases, separated by long kilometers of barren wasteland.

With summer temperatures reaching 54C and humidity extremely high, Bartholomew apparently spent time preaching at many of these large oases, some of which supported up to nine or ten villages of mainly mud huts. Bartholomew seems to have spent up to twelve years faithfully preaching the gospel throughout this inhospitable land.

Later accounts claim that Christianity was planted in Arabia in the first half of the first century. In Mohammed's time large settlements of Christians with their own bishops, churches and monasteries were well established in most of the leading towns of Arabia, although there is no record of a Christian community in Mecca itself.

From the Iranian account, it would seem that Bartholomew then spent some time preaching throughout southern Persia, before apparently returning to Jerusalem for the Passover of 44AD. He may have been there when James the Greater was beheaded by Herod and Peter was miraculously released from prison.

It may also be that at this time he met up with Jude Thaddaeus who had spent the previous eight years ministering in Armenia. After reporting on his missionary activities to the Jerusalem church, Bartholomew seems to have obtained one or two copies of Matthew's gospel in Hebrew or Aramaic. Either he or Jude Thaddaeus apparently took a copy to Edessa at this time, as Jerome says the church there still had an original copy of Matthew's gospel in Hebrew three centuries later.

## ARMENIA

After leaving Jerusalem, Bartholomew then proceeded to Armenia[4] where Armenian sources claim he spent sixteen years all told ministering for the Lord, much of it in the first half of the first century AD. Armenian church annals claim Jude Thaddaeus and Bartholomew as the founders of the church in their country.

Bartholomew is said to have arrived in Armenia in 44AD where he apparently spent the next ten years preaching the gospel and praying for the sick. Towards the end of his stay, possibly around 52AD, Bartholomew was joined by Andrew and the two apostles served the Lord together there for about two years.

According to Budge, in The Preaching of St Andrew and St Bartholomew, the two are then said to have laboured amongst the Parthians for a time.[5]

In the spring of 57AD, Andrew seems to have returned to Armenia while, as Jerome, the Roman Martyrology, the Iranian church and other sources state,  Bartholomew  continued on along the main highway into India.[6]

## INDIA

Travelling along the centuries-old trade route from Mashad to Bactria, Bartholomew would have then crossed the Khyber Pass to reach Taxila, capital of Gandhara,  junction of three major  trade routes and now under Kushan rule.

About ten years previously Thomas had spent quite some time in Taxila successfully preaching the gospel to its inhabitants. Bartholomew would no doubt have sought to strengthen and encourage these believers before he moved on.

William Carey states that Bartholomew eventually reached a Jewish colony on the far side of the Ganges River.  After winning many to the Lord, Bartholomew left with them one of his precious copies of Matthew's gospel in Aramaic.

Eusebius and Jerome both relate that in 180AD, Demetrius, Bishop of Alexandria, sent Pantaenus, a leading Christian teacher of the church there, as a missionary to India.   Jerome adds that he was to preach to the Brahmins there, which would seem to confirm that the Indian sub-continent was his destination.

When Pantaenus arrived in India, he discovered descendants of Bartholomew's original converts who were still faithful to the Lord. They showed him the gospel of Matthew in Hebrew characters which Bartholomew had left with them.  On his return to Alexandria Pantaenus brought this gospel  back with him.

From India Bartholomew is said to have taken ship to Egypt and spent some months preaching there.

## ARMENIA

Early in 60AD Bartholomew joined Jude Thaddaeus, Simon the Zealot and Andrew back in Armenia.[7]  The four apostles worked together for a short time before Simon left for Britain and Andrew for Asia Minor.

The Armenian church claims that Bartholomew and Jude Thaddaeus then spent the next six years preaching the gospel in Greater Armenia.

Bartholomew was apparently not with Jude Thaddaeus when he,

with around one thousand other Christians was martyred on the 28th October, 66AD at Ardaz, near Mt Ararat, in south eastern Armenia.

## HIERAPOLIS

It was probably early in 67AD that Bartholomew is said by Chrysostom and in the Acts of Philip to have joined his old friend Philip at Hierapolis.[8]

The two apostles ministered together here for several months. During this time the wife of the proconsul was healed and became a dedicated Christian.

This so infuriated the proconsul that he had Philip and Bartholomew arrested and imprisoned.

At first both were sentenced to be crucified, but for some reason, at the last minute, Bartholomew was released. Philip, however, was brutally pierced through the ankles and thighs and fastened upside down to a cross, before being stoned to death, as Nicephorus tells us, on the 15th November of probably 67AD.

After the death of his friend, Bartholomew made his way into Lycaonia,[9] where Chrysostom states that he preached and taught the people for some months, before returning to Armenia in the summer of 68AD.

## DEATH AT ALBANOPOLIS

The place of Bartholomew's martyrdom is attested to by various writers, however the Apostolic History of Abdias gives us the possible lead up to it.

Abdias tells us that Bartholomew came to a town, later identified as Albanopolis,[10] where there was a temple of Astaroth. The idol there suddenly ceased to answer his worshippers. So they went to another city and inquired of Beireth who told them Bartholomew was the cause.

For two days the people could not find him. Then Bartholomew cast a devil out of a man. King Polymius heard of it and sent for him to heal his lunatic daughter who bit everyone. She was immediately loosed from her affliction and totally cured.

The king sent camels laden with riches, but the apostle could not be found. Next day, however, he came to the king and expounded the Christian faith, then offered to show him the demon who inhabited his idol.   Bartholomew bade the demon leave the idol, and the statue immediately fell to the ground and broke.

The king and all his family believed and were   baptised. The heathen priests, however, were incensed.  They went and complained to the king's brother, Astyages, who had Bartholomew bound and brought to him.  After  questioning Bartholomew, Astyages had him beaten with clubs, flayed and crucified.

The people mourned Bartholomew, and buried him with great honour,  building an impressive basilica over his tomb.  After twenty days Astyages was seized by a devil and died. Great fear came over the people and many believed in Christ. The king, Polymius, became bishop of the church there and presided over it for twenty years.

This is said by numerous writers to have taken place at Albanopolis at the foot of the Caucasus Mountains on the west coast of the Caspian Sea.

This town was the sea gate through which the wild horsemen of the Steppes, (Scythians, Huns and Khazars), rode down upon civilised communities.   It is now called Derbend and is situated  in the area known as Azerbaijan.   .

The date of Bartholomew's death is said to be the 24th August 68 AD. Thus, the two friends who were among the first to give their allegiance to Christ, sealed their devotion with their lives. They entered into their eternal reward  within less than a year of each other, after more than thirty-five years of fruitful ministry for their Lord.

## REFERENCES FOR BARTHOLOMEW

1.   John 1:45-51, Fig tree : Fausset p 78, Barclay pp 108-109, McBirnie p 130, Genesis 28:12,  John 2:1-11, 4:46-54, 21:2,  Halley pp 533,537

2.   James pp 468-469

3.   Acts 2:11, McBirnie p 130, 133, Fausset p 78, 236, Latourette p 107, Smiley pp 9, 62, 104, 105, John 1:28, Jackson p 42, II Chronicles 8:17-18,   Unger (A:OT) pp 86, 99, 117, 222-227, Matthew 12:42, Luke 11:31,  Hazard pp11-13,41-46,55-59,  Int Std Bible Enc Vol I, p 222, 224, 433, (Budge 11.90), Isaiah 60:6, Jeremiah 6:20, Ezekiel 27:22, Psalm 72:10, Luke 1:10,  I Kings 9:26-28, 10:1,2,10,13,22,  Genesis 37:25, Exodus 30:7-8, 22-33, Enc Brit Vol VII, p 151, 17/502, Edersheim p 13

4.  McBirnie pp 130-141, Barclay pp 102-105
5.  McBirnie pp 130,131,133, Halley p 466, Int Std Bible Enc Vol I p 433 (Budge 11.83)
6.  Barclay p 104, McBirnie pp 130, 133, 134, 140,  Fox (B) p 6, Latourette pp101, 107,  Anti-Nicene Fathers (Jerome) p 370, Eusebius(W) pp 213-214, William Carey p 230, Wenham p 117, Henry p 552, Atiya p 52, Edersheim p 13
7.  McBirnie p 133, James pp 466
8.  Barclay p 104, McBirnie p 130,131`, 140
9.  McBirnie pp 131 (Chrysostom), 141, James p 449
10. McBirnie p 140, 199, Atiya p 316, Barclay p104,  James p 468, Fox (B) p 6

# THREE APOSTLES NAMED JAMES

In the writings of the early church confusion often arose over the fact that there were three apostles named James in the New Testament. Probably the best known of the three was **James the Greater,** so called either because of his age or size, or as is more probable, because of his importance and position within the twelve.

Next came **James the Less,** so designated because of his inferior position to James the greater in either age, size or position. Both were members of the original twelve.[1]

Thirdly, there was **James the brother of Jesus.** Although James, along with his brothers, did not believe on Jesus until after the resurrection, his transformation and dedication were so great that he was made leader of the church in Jerusalem. It was to him that the apostles reported on their return from various missionary endeavours.[2]

Although some traditions confuse one with the other, it is possible, by linking the information in the scriptures with that found elsewhere, to form a reasonably accurate picture of the life and work of all three.

## JAMES THE GREATER

Son of Zebedee and Salome and elder brother of the apostle John, James[3] was one of the early disciples to receive the call from Jesus to follow Him. A fisherman of Capernaum, James and his family were sufficiently wealthy to employ hired servants to assist them in their fishing business.

James was probably brought to the Lord by his younger brother John very soon after John and Andrew spent their memorable day talking with Jesus. James is mentioned as being present early in Jesus'

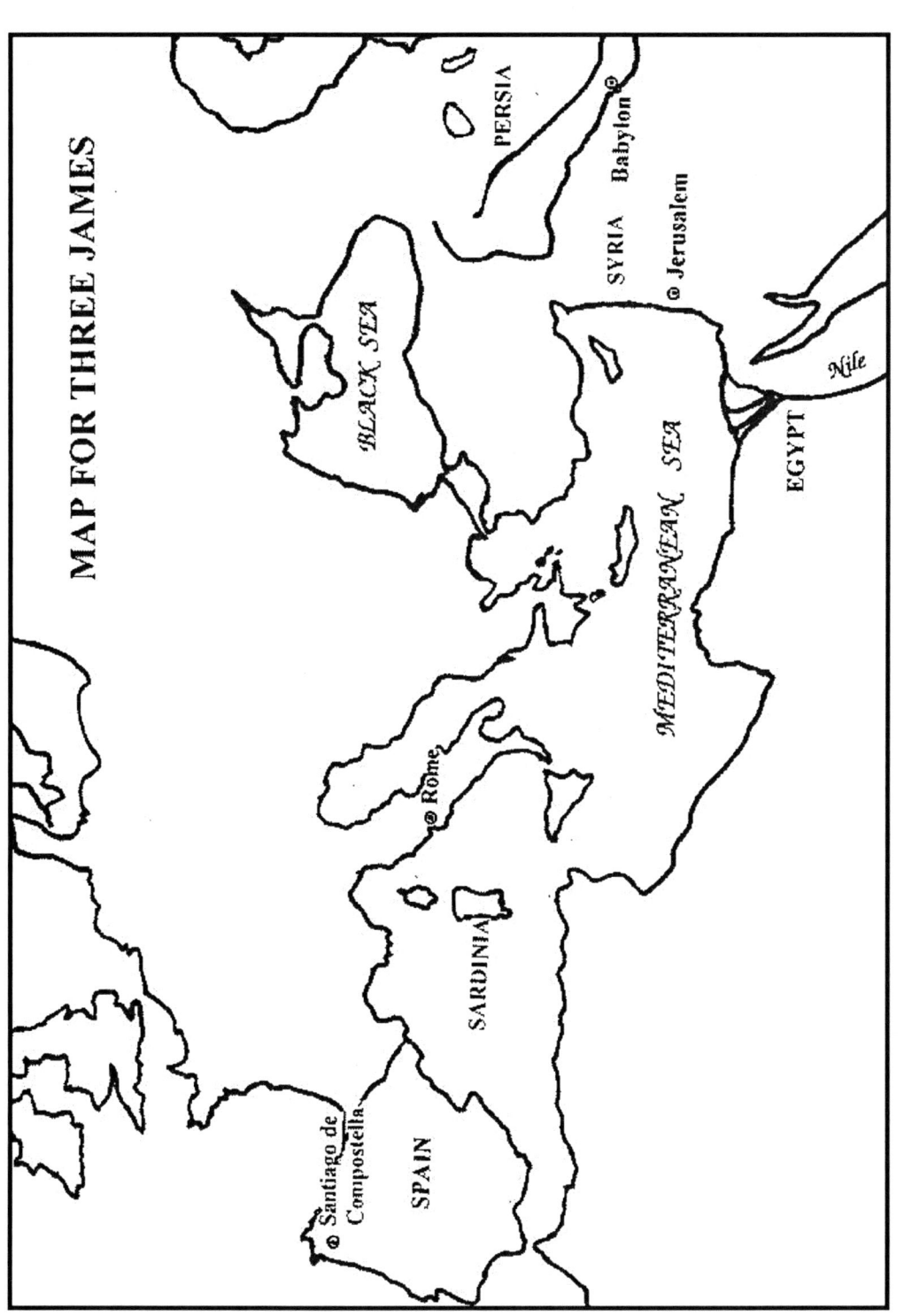

MAP FOR THREE JAMES

ministry when Jesus healed Peter's mother-in-law at Capernaum.

At one stage James and John wanted to call down fire on the people of a small Samaritan village who had refused to allow Jesus and his disciples lodging for the night. Jesus rebuked them, but it was probably this hot-headedness in the brothers that had earlier caused Jesus to name them "Sons of Thunder".

## SALOME

Salome,[4] their mother, was among the women who followed Jesus, and provided for Him and his disciples out of their own means. She seems to have been a rather strong-willed woman. On their last journey to Jerusalem, Jesus had just told his disciples that he was going to suffer and die and on the third day rise again.

Without apparently taking in the enormity of what Jesus had just told them, Salome asked the Lord to grant that her two sons be given the privilege of sitting on His right and left hand when He came into His kingdom. Jesus told her that she didn't know what she was asking, and that the honour was not His to give. This incident certainly put the two brothers off-side with the rest of the disciples.

Salome proved her faithfulness, however, by remaining at the cross with her son John, Mary and the other women when all hope of an earthly kingdom seemed to be lost. Then on the first day of the week she was one of those who went to the tomb at daybreak to minister to the body of Jesus, only to discover that He had indeed risen from the dead as He had told them.

## TRAINING OF JAMES

James[5] was one of the four who questioned the Lord concerning the last things when Jesus delivered His address on the Mount of Olives as they stood over-looking the Temple. He was also one of the seven who went fishing in the Sea of Tiberias after the resurrection.

But one of the puzzling things about James, considering the shortness of his ministry, is that he was one of the inner three, along with Peter and John, to receive special training from Jesus.

Only these three were present when Jesus restored the daughter of Jairus to life. Then, towards the end of Jesus' ministry, James was one of the same three to witness the Lord's amazing transformation on the mountain, when Moses and Elijah talked with Him about His coming death.

Finally, in the Garden of Gethsemane, Jesus took Peter, James and John apart from the rest of the disciples and asked them to watch with Him as He wrestled alone with the Father in anguished prayer.

From all of this, we would expect to see James exercising a ministry almost as important as that of Peter, and certainly as great as his younger brother, John. In the book of Acts, however, there is no mention of James the Greater from the Day of Pentecost until the brief account of his death some fourteen years later.

Where was James when Peter and John were fearlessly preaching the gospel to the multitudes, healing the lame man at the gate beautiful, or bravely informing the Sanhedrin that they had to obey God rather than men?

Yet if James had done so little to attract attention to himself, it seems strange that Herod, in his efforts to please the Jews, would have singled out James, rather than one of the other apostles, for execution.

## SPAIN AND SARDINIA

Although the book of Acts remains silent on the matter, many early traditions state that not long after the Day of Pentecost, possibly soon after the stoning of Stephen, James left Jerusalem to take the gospel to colonies of Jews working as slaves on the island of Sardinia and in the mines of Spain.[6]

Both Tacitus and Josephus mention that four thousand young Jews had been transported from Rome to Sardinia in 19AD for forcible enlistment as soldiers. Many were later sent to work in the mines of both Sardinia and Spain. It is believed that quite a number of these banished Jews were formerly followers of Judas the Galilean, who were taken to Rome as prisoners in 6AD. If so, they would have come from the area around Galilee and may have been known to the families of the apostles.

It is possible that the relatives of these men had pleaded with Jesus, while He was still with them, to send this new message to their sons in captivity. If this was the case, James could have been appointed by the Saviour Himself to fulfil this commitment.

There are various later accounts of James having worked tirelessly in both places and he is credited with having founded many churches in Spain.

Isidore of Seville, writing in the seventh century, stated, "James the son of Zebedee and the brother of John ... preached the gospel to Spain and the peoples of the West."

The Venerable Bede (673-735) in his Ecclesiastical History of the English People, wrote, "Peter received for share Rome, Andrew Achaia, James Spain and Thomas India."

The ministry of James the Greater in Spain is also mentioned by Julian of Toledo in the seventh century, by Freculpus who wrote about 850AD and in the writings of the Bollandists. These writers apparently based their accounts on references in old Spanish Offices, and on generally accepted local traditions.

The Apostolic History of Abdias has a somewhat unusual story about James the Greater and two magicians named Hermogenes and Philetus.

In the course of James' preaching, presumably in Spain, he is said to have been opposed by Hermogenes and Philetus. Philetus was eventually converted to Christ and informed Hermogenes that he was leaving him. Hermogenes bound him fast by magical incantations and said, "We will see if James can free you." Philetus succeeded in getting a servant to take a message to James, who sent his kerchief back and by its influence Philetus was freed and escaped to James.

In time Hermogenes, too, was converted and destroyed all his magical books. James sent him to undo his former works where possible and to spend in charity what he had gained by his magical acts. Hermogenes obeyed and grew in faith to such an extent that he too performed miracles.

Cressy in his Church History of Britanny quotes Flavius Dexter as follows, "In the one and fortieth year of Christ St James, returning out of Spain visited Gaul, Brittany and the towns of the Venetians where he preached the gospel and so came back to Jerusalem to consult with ... St Peter about matters of very great weight and importance."

James returned to Jerusalem just before Passover of 44AD. Abdias tells us that the Jews bribed two centurions, Lysias and Theocritus to seize James. As he was being taken away, James spoke to the people about Christ and the judgement of God. The people cried out, "We have sinned."

Abiathar the high priest stirred up a tumult and a scribe cast a rope about James' neck and they dragged him before Herod.

## HEROD AGRIPPA I

This was Herod Agrippa I[7], grandson of Herod the Great. Under Caligula, Agrippa had been appointed governor of the former tetrachies of Philip and Lysanias. On the exile of Herod Antipas in 39AD, Galilee and Perea were added to his dominions. Then in 41AD, because of Agrippa's services to the new emperor, Claudius, Judaea and Samaria were also placed under his rule. Agrippa now controlled exactly the same kingdom as his grandfather had, and was accorded the title of king. This gave him the authority to inflict the death sentence on anyone who annoyed him sufficiently.

His power was short-lived, however. Shortly after the death of James, in the fourth year of Agrippa's reign over the whole kingdom, he suddenly met an untimely end. At the beginning of August 44AD Herod Agrippa attended games at Caesarea to celebrate the safe return of the emperor Claudius from his invasion of Britain.

Josephus tells us that Herod appeared in the theatre in a robe of silver which shone with a dazzling brightness in the morning light. Luke tells us that after he delivered a public address to the people, they shouted, "This is the voice of a god, not of a man."

Immediately, Herod was struck with a violent pain in his bowels and died in agony five days later at the age of fifty-three.

## DEATH OF JAMES

Herod may have previously received reports from the Jewish leaders in Spain telling of James' preaching to the slaves there and in Sardinia.

Wanting to please the Jews, as Luke tells us in Acts, Herod could well have accused James of stirring up sedition in those places, and have used this as an excuse to impose the death sentence.[8]

` On his way to Herod, James is said to have healed a paralytic. The scribe, Josias, who was leading James to judgement, was convicted both by the preaching of James and by witnessing this healing. He begged James to forgive him.

After considering a little, James said, "Peace be with you," and kissed him. Water was brought and James baptized him. Abiathar, the high priest, then had Josias beheaded along with James.

Slightly different versions of this story are told by both Abdias and

Clement of Alexandria. Clement's account is recorded in Eusebius.

After the execution, Abdias tells us, Hermogenes and Philetus retrieved James' body and embarking at Joppa, immediately sailed for Spain. They landed at a place called Iria Flavia, today known as El Padron, where James' body was interred.

In the ninth century the body of James is said to have been removed from Iria Flavia by King Alphonso the Chaste and taken to Santiago de Compostella where pilgrims visit his shrine to this day.

Many of the later accounts of James' ministry in Spain contain stories of the Virgin Mary appearing to the apostle and assisting him in various ways. This led to protestants generally rejecting the whole concept of James preaching in Spain.

However, the Encyclopaedia Britannica affirms James' martyrdom fourteen years after the death of Christ, in 44AD, by order of Herod Agrippa I of Judaea, grandson of Herod the Great. It adds, "According to Spanish tradition, his body was transported to Santiago de Compostella where his shrine attracts pilgrims from all over the world."

James was later named patron saint of Spain. In early sacred art he is depicted with a copy of the gospel in one hand and a pilgrim staff and scrip in the other to show symbolically how far-travelled an evangelist he was.

First of the apostles to die, James is the only one, other than Judas, whose death is reported in the New Testament.

James was probably around fifty years of age at the time of his death. This was about half the age of his younger brother John who died more than fifty years later at around one hundred years of age.

So the apostle who seems at first glance to have done the least in the service of his Master may actually have spent those fourteen years after the resurrection in wholehearted and devoted missionary service for his Lord.

## REFERENCES FOR JAMES THE GREATER
1.  Matthew 10:2-4, McBirnie pp 185-187, Unger (Dict) pp 552-553, IVP Bible Dict Pt 2 p 732
2.  Matthew 13:55, Mark 6:3, John 7:5, Acts 1:14, 12:17, 15:13, Galatians 1:19, 2:9
3.  Matt 4:18, 21,22, Mark 1:16-20, 29-31, 3:17, Luke 9:51-56

4. Luke 8:1-3, Matthew 20:20-28, Mark 15:40-41, 16:1
5. Mark 13:3-4, John 21:1-3, Mark 5:22,37, Matthew 17:1-3, Mark 9:2, Matthew 26:36-38, Acts 1:13, 12:1-3
6. Tacitus 'Annals, vol ii, c.85', Lewis pp 89-90, DeSouza p 16, Josephus 'Antiquities' Bk xviii, cap 3, Acts 5:37, Barclay p 99, Taylor pp 56-58, McBirnie pp 103, 107, James p 463, Latourette p 96
7. Acts 12:1,19-23, Josephus Antiquities Bk XIX : 8, Fausset pp 285-286, Eusebius (W) pp 81-83,
8. James pp 463-464, Eusebius (W) pp 81-82 (Clement), Fausset p 326, Acts 12:1-3, McBirnie p 90, 104-107, Barclay p 98, 100, Enc Brittanica Volume V p 508, Fox (Z) p 2

## JAMES THE LESS

James the Less, ('ho mikros' - the little or younger) is a rather shadowy figure both in the New Testament and also in the records of tradition. He is always mentioned about half-way down the list of apostles, where he is called 'James the son of Alphaeus'.[1] Matthew is also designated 'the son of Alphaeus' and it has been conjectured that the two may have been brothers. Alphaeus was a fairly common name in Palestine at that time, though and it seems unlikely they were related.

We are told by both Matthew and Mark, however, that James the Less did have a brother and his name was Joses. According to Eusebius he apparently also had a much younger brother named Simon or Symeon.

James the Less was a native of Capernaum on the north-west shore of the Sea of Galilee. He is said to have been of the tribe of Gad.

### MOTHER

His mother, Mary[2], was one of those women who followed Jesus and ministered to him during his travels. In John's gospel we are told, "Near the cross of Jesus stood his mother, his mother's sister, Mary the wife of Clopas, and Mary Magdalene." Matthew and Mark both state that the second Mary was the mother of James the Less (or younger) and of Joses.

Luke tells us that this Mary was one of the women who took spices to the tomb early on the first day of the week. When the women returned in haste and told the disciples the message of the two angels, that Jesus had indeed risen from the dead, their words were treated as idle tales or nonsense.

Some confusion has existed over the fact that James was said to be the son of Alphaeus whereas Mary was the wife of Clopas. However all is clear when we find that Clopas is the Hebrew form of the Greek name Alphaeus.

Another question has been posed as to why two sisters would both have the name Mary. Unger and others mention an early account which states that, rather than being sisters, the two were actually sisters-in-law, with Clopas being the brother of Mary's husband, Joseph.

Eusebius states that the Symeon who became leader of the Jerusalem church on the death of James the Just, was the son of the Clopas mentioned by John. He adds, "Hegesippus tells us that Clopas was Joseph's brother."

## MINISTRY OF JAMES

As far as James himself is concerned, there is very little recorded, even in apocryphal literature, of his later ministry.[3] He is said to have preached in both Palestine and Persia. In his History of Eastern Christianity, Aziz S Atiya relates that the Syrian Church claims James the Less as its first bishop.

Halley, Schofield and others state that James then travelled down to Egypt. After ministering there for some time, this lesser-known apostle finally sealed his testimony for his Lord and Saviour by dying a martyr's death on a cross.

## REFERENCES FOR JAMES THE LESS

1. Matthew 10:1-4, Mark 3:13-19, Luke 6:12-16, Acts 1:13, Matthew 27:56, McBirnie p 184, IVP Bible Dict Pt 2 p 732
2. Matthew 27:56,61, Mark 15:40,41, 47, 16:1, Luke 24:1-11, John 19:25, Unger (Dict) p 553, Eusebius(W) pp 123-124, 181
3. Atiya p 239, McBirnie p 193, Barclay p 114, Halley p 466, Schofield pp 15-16, Thompson's NIV p 1565

## JAMES THE BROTHER OF JESUS

Much of the confusion in separating the ministries of James the son of Zebedee, James the son of Alphaeus and James the brother of Jesus arose from early attempts to establish the perpetual virginity of Mary. However, as Unger and others state, the literal interpretation of Matthew 13:55, Mark 6:3 and other scriptures is that those mentioned were the natural sons and daughters of Joseph and Mary.[1]

To avoid admitting this, some early writers decided that the James mentioned as the brother of Jesus was James the Less, a cousin of Jesus. But problems arise when we read in John that even towards the end of Jesus' earthly ministry his brothers did not believe on Him. To have been one of the twelve, James the Less had to have been with Jesus from the beginning of His ministry. Therefore they could not have been one and the same person.[2]

### FAMILY

Luke calls Jesus Mary's 'first-born' - prototokos - rather than monogenes, the term which would be used for an only child, indicating that Jesus was the first in a family.[3]  Born about two years after Jesus, James was the eldest of four other brothers and at least three sisters.

Both Matthew and Mark tell us that after Jesus  preached in the synagogue at Nazareth, the townspeople were greatly divided in their opinion of Him. Some were amazed at his teaching. Others felt Jesus was just one of their village men.

"Isn't this the carpenter's son?" they exclaimed. "Isn't his mother's name Mary, and aren't his brothers James, Joseph, Simon and Judas?  Aren't all his sisters, with us?" In Mark the townspeople called Jesus 'the carpenter',  indicating that he had taken over the family's carpenter shop after the death of Joseph. And in the list of brothers Judas is mentioned before Simon.

This Judas, or Jude is the author of the epistle which appears in our New Testament just before the book of Revelation. In  it he introduces himself as 'a servant of Jesus Christ and brother of James', as if James was an important and well-known figure.

James would have been around twenty-eight when Jesus began his public ministry, with the rest of the family  ranging in age probably down to their late teens. As Matthew mentions 'all' of the girls, it would seem there were at least three sisters.

The apocryphal History of Joseph names two of them as Lydia and Lysia. Apparently they had all married and settled in Nazareth.

From Paul's comments in his letter to the Corinthians it would appear that all the brothers of Jesus, including James, were also married.

## JAMES

James was dedicated to God from his birth, and by all accounts had led a very studious and holy life, even as a child and young man.

He seems to have resented the more easy-going relationship Jesus had with God, compared with his own strict religious observances. Early in his life, Hegesippus tells us, James took the vow of a Nazarite,[4] pledging never to drink wine or strong drink, nor to have his hair cut.

Apparently neither Mary nor Joseph had told anyone of the visits of the angels or wise men, nor the fact that Jesus was to be the promised Messiah. Early writers state that, in view of Daniel's prophecy, people at that time were looking expectantly for the appearance of the messiah. Therefore it would have seemed presumptuous for Mary to claim that her son was the chosen one. She probably also wanted Jesus to grow up as normally as possible and was prepared to wait for God to bring him forth in His own time.

It was not until after the resurrection that Mary apparently told James and the rest of the family about Jesus.

Jerome and Hegesippus, quoting from the Gospel According to the Hebrews, relate that when James finally learnt the truth, he made a vow to neither eat nor drink until Jesus should appear to him personally.

Paul tells us in Corinthians that Jesus did indeed appear to James sometime after His appearance to the five hundred in Galilee.

From the other account we learn that Jesus said to James, "My brother, eat thy bread, for the Son of Man is risen from among them that sleep." Then, Clement of Alexander tells us, Jesus imparted to James the higher knowledge, and explained to him the true meaning of His life and death.[5]

James, his mother and brothers were among the one hundred and twenty filled with the Holy Spirit on the Day of Pentecost. Following this, Eusebius tells us, the apostles met together and chose James to be the leader of the church in Jerusalem, a position he held until the day of his martyrdom thirty-two years later.[6]

## EPISTLE

Matthew had already written his gospel in Hebrew, possibly around 37AD, to show the Jews that Jesus was indeed their long awaited Messiah. Mark' s gospel had also been written in Rome for the Romans about 45 AD. Then, around 47AD, some time before the first of Paul's letters and apparently before the Council of 49AD, James wrote his pastoral epistle[7] directed to the Christians scattered abroad amongst the twelve tribes of Israel.

His aim was to give the newly-formed Christian communities practical guide-lines for Christian living, possibly in response to questions raised when the various groups visited Jerusalem for the Jewish festivals each year.

The epistle contains much teaching similar to Jesus' sermon on the mount. From this it has been conjectured that, even though James could have gleaned the information from Matthew's gospel, it is also possible that he may have been among the crowd when Jesus first delivered these precepts.

While not accepting Jesus' other claims, James may have been deeply impressed with Jesus' teaching on holy living.

## LEADERSHIP

James seems to have given wise and strong leadership[8] to the young church. Even the other apostles appear to have looked up to him and respected his decisions. At the council of 49AD when the vexed question of whether Gentile Christians should keep the law of Moses and be circumcised, James encouraged Peter, Paul, Barnabas and others to give their views.

Then James spoke up, quoting the Old Testament to back up his views. He concluded by saying, "It is my judgement, therefore, that we should not make it difficult for the Gentiles who are turning to God ..."

In the letter he sent to the Gentile Christians at Antioch, he said, "It seemed good to the Holy Spirit and to us not to burden you..."

For a strict Jew like James, his tolerant summing up of the situation showed a great measure of wisdom, maturity and also humility.

Luke tells us that James' words pleased the apostles and elders and the whole church to the extent that they sent a letter expressing these views for Judas and Silas to read to the new Christians at Antioch.

Earlier, when Peter was miraculously released from prison, he hurried to the home of John Mark, and after relating what had happened, he asked them to let James know.

## PAUL

Each time Paul returned to Jerusalem, he apparently reported his activities to James, and was guided by James' advice in what he did. Paul had no hesitation in putting Peter in his place when he felt he was wrong, yet there is no indication that he ever disputed personally with James. For a man of Paul's temperament, this would seem to indicate his deep respect and appreciation for the fine character and strong leadership James exhibited.

On Paul's last visit to Jerusalem, James said to him, "You see, brother, how many thousands of Jews there are which believe..." and he encouraged Paul to go with four other men to a service of purification in the temple to show the Jews that he still observed the laws of Moses.

This led to the Jews clamouring for Paul's arrest and his subsequent night-time escape to Caesarea after a tip off from his nephew that the Jewish leaders had taken a vow to kill him.

## MARTYRDOM OF JAMES

Although James was the undisputed leader of the Jerusalem church, he lived such a holy and virtuous life that he was surnamed James the Just or James the Righteous by the Jewish people at large.

Hegesippus tells us that James wore only linen clothes such as the priests wore, and because of his Nazarite vow and his holy life, he was allowed to go daily into the holy place of the temple.

Here he would spend hours on his knees interceding for the nation of Israel. Eventually, says Hegesippus, James' knees became calloused like those of a camel.

In spite of this, the Jewish leaders, having been thwarted in their attempt to have Paul executed, now turned their attention to James.[9]

Their chance came, we are told by Josephus and others, when in 62AD, Festus, the Roman Procurator who had interrogated Paul at Caesarea, died in office. In the interval of about two months before his successor could arrive, Annus the high priest decided to take matters into his own hands.

He had sixty-four year old James brought before the Sanhedrin for supposedly breaking the law.

It was the time of the Passover, with millions of Jews in Jerusalem. Annus gave James the chance to save himself. He instructed him to stand on the pinnacle of the temple, 450ft above the Kidron Valley, and tell the people that Jesus was not the Christ. Because he was respected by all the people, the leaders said, they would believe what he said.

However, standing high on the pinnacle before all the people, James shouted, "Why do you ask me concerning Jesus, the Son of Man? He sits at the right hand of power and will come again on the clouds of heaven." Many cried out, "Hosanna to the Son of David," and believed on Jesus.

The leaders said to each other, "We had better go up and throw him down, so that they will be frightened and not believe him."

"Ho! Ho!" they called out, "Even the Righteous One has gone astray!" So they cast him down and as he was still alive in spite of his fall, they began to stone him. But James turned and knelt, uttering the words, "I beseech Thee, Lord God and Father, forgive them, they do not know what they are doing."

A descendant of Rechab called out, "Stop what you are doing! The Righteous One is praying for you!" But a fuller took the club which he used at the nearby laundry and brought it down on the head of James and killed him. James the Righteous was buried near the spot where he died and his head-stone is still there by the sanctuary.

Josephus, the Jewish historian, later wrote that the Jewish people believed that the terrible things which happened to them in the four year war with Rome, ending in the total destruction of Jerusalem, was in requital for the way they had put to death 'James the brother of Christ, who was the most righteous of men'.

After James' death, his younger cousin Symeon,[10] son of Clopas, the brother of James' father, Joseph, was appointed to lead the

Jerusalem church.   He, too, was  martyred for his faith under Trajan in 107AD.

## REFERENCES FOR JAMES THE BROTHER OF JESUS

1.  Unger (Dict) p 553,  McBirnie pp 185-186,  Psalm 69:8, Matthew 1:25, 12:46-50,  Mark 3:31-35,  Luke 8:19-21, Galatians 1:19, 2:9, I Corinthians 9:5

2.  Matthew 10:3,  Mark 3:18,  Luke 6:15,  John 7:1-5,  Acts 1:21-22

3.  Luke 2:7, Mathew 13:56, Mark 6:3, James p 84,  I Corinthians 9:5,

4.  Numbers 4:1-5,  Eusebius (W) pp 99-103,  Barclay p 81, McBirnie p 191,  Unger (Dict)  p 553,  Halley p 657,  John 7:3-5

5.  Eusebius (W) p 72,  Barclay p 82-83,   I Corinthians 15:5-7, FF Bruce (NT:Hist) pp 350-353

6.  Acts 1:14,  Eusebius (W) p 72, 118

7.  Unger (Dict) p 553,  Fausset p 327,  Schofield p 1306,  Hunter p 236-239, 8 Acts 12:17, 15:13,19, 21:17-26, McBirnie pp 187-190,

8.  Josephus : Antiquities Book 20:9.1, Barclay pp 80-81, Halley p 657, Eusebius (W) pp 99-103,  Galatians 2:9

9.  Eusebius(W) p 102, Josephus :  Ant  (Appendix pp 815-816), FF Bruce (Men) pp 110-116, Foxe (B) p 8

10. Eusebius(W) pp 123-124, 181, John 19:25, Morton (M) pp 53-54, 58

# MATTHEW

In Matthew's own gospel he tells us that 'As Jesus went on from there, he saw a man named Matthew,[1] sitting at the tax collector's booth. "Follow me," he told him, and Matthew got up and followed him.'

Both Mark and Luke, in reporting the same incident, call the man Levi, and Mark adds that he was the son of Alphaeus. It was the custom in Palestine for men to have two names. Matthew means 'the gift of God', and the name Levi may indicate that he was from that tribe.

The main fact about Matthew-Levi, however, was that he was a tax collector. The Authorised Version of the Bible calls him a publican, from the Latin word publicanus, or a man who was engaged in public service. No class of men in the ancient world was more hated or despised than tax collectors.

William Barclay states, "Of all nations the Jews were the most vigorous haters of tax collectors. For a strict Jew God was the only person to whom it was right to pay tribute.

"A tax gatherer was debarred from being either a witness or a judge. He was even debarred from worship, which was why the tax gatherer in the parable stood afar off.

"Under the Roman system of tax collecting, the responsibility was given to various local officers. For the purposes of government Palestine was divided into two. Samaria and Judaea in the south were directly under a Roman procurator, but Galilee in the north was ruled by Herod Antipas, subject to the Romans. Matthew, therefore, was not in the service of the Romans but of Herod Antipas, who was in any case, just a vassal of Rome.

"Matthew's position was a frontier post. The great Road of the East came from Damascus to the Mediterranean sea-port of Acre. It first passed through the territory of Iturea and Trachonitis, which belonged to Philip, Herod's brother, then at Capernaum it entered

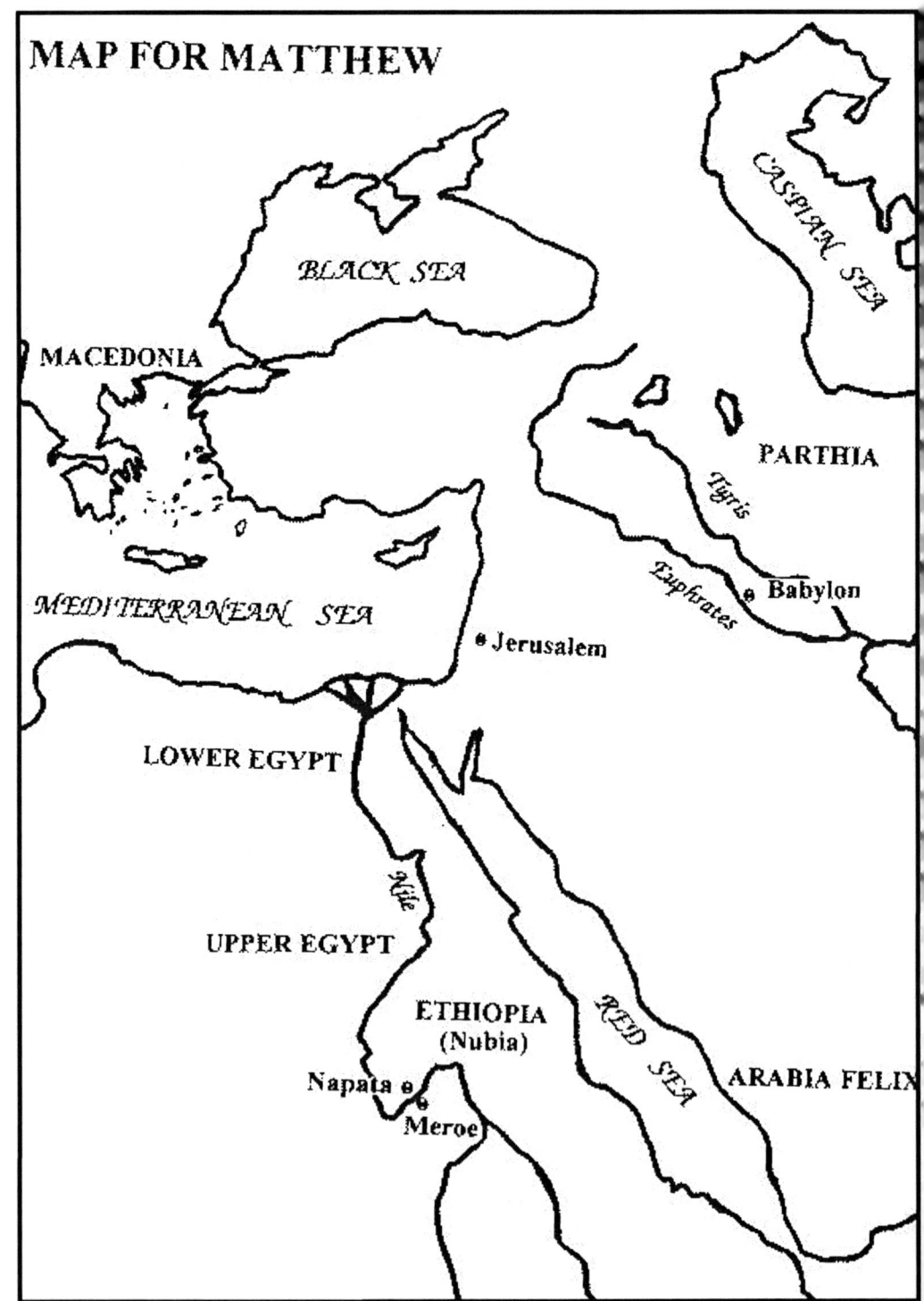

MAP FOR MATTHEW

CASPIAN SEA

BLACK SEA

MACEDONIA

PARTHIA

Tigris

Euphrates

Babylon

MEDITERRANEAN SEA

Jerusalem

LOWER EGYPT

Nile

UPPER EGYPT

ETHIOPIA
(Nubia)

RED SEA

ARABIA FELIX

Napata

Meroe

Galilee and the territory of Herod. It was probably with the traffic on that road and the traffic on the Sea of Galilee itself, that Matthew was concerned."

From his customs booth near the sea-shore at Capernaum, Matthew must have often heard Jesus preaching to the multitudes that thronged Him. He would also have heard many stories of the dramatic healings that had taken place in the town. Matthew may even have witnessed Jesus calling Peter, Andrew, James and John to leave their fishing nets and follow Him.

 Matthew's heart must have been deeply stirred by it all. Then one day Jesus Himself stood before Matthew - the despised, ostracised publican - and said quietly, but with authority, "Follow Me!" Matthew's heart was ready to obey. Immediately he gladly left all and followed Jesus.

The first thing Matthew did  was to give a lavish feast in his own home for the only friends he had, his fellow tax collectors and other outcasts from society, so that they, too, could have the chance to meet Jesus personally. The scribes and Pharisees were shocked that Jesus should eat with such company, but Jesus' answer was, "It is not the healthy who need a doctor, but the sick."

Matthew must have been quite wealthy to own a house large enough to hold the crowd and to afford such a lavish feast.   Yet he seems to have never wavered in his decision to leave it all behind to follow Jesus.

## SAYINGS

There was something from his old life, however, that Matthew took into his new life with Jesus.   That was his pen and his ability to write, both in his native Hebrew (or Aramaic) and in Greek.

As a tax collector Matthew would also have had to learn a form of shorthand[2] with which to write down quick assessments of the consignments before him.

Early shorthand was invented by Marcus Tiro, a learned freedman of Cicero's household. In 63BC Tiro devised a system for taking down the speeches made by men like Cicero and later Seneca in the Roman Senate.

His system was considered so good that it was taught in Roman schools and was in use for over one thousand years. Most of the

Roman emperors from the time of Julius Caesar were proficient in it. It was also extensively used in later years by many Christian bishops and church authorities. Origen is said to have used up to seven shorthand writers in rotation to take down his prolific output of literature.

In Tiro's day the notes were written on an ivory tablet with a sharp stylus. Matthew may have used a wax tablet from which the day's writing could be easily erased after being transcribed.

In this way Matthew is thought to have written down much of Jesus' teaching, including the sermon on the mount, His many parables and other observations as they occurred day by day.

Among the three thousand new converts on the Day of Pentecost were representatives from at least fifteen different nations. These new believers needed something in the form of written teaching to take back with them to their homelands.

To meet this need, Papias tells us, "Matthew compiled the Sayings[3] (oracles or logia) of the Lord in Aramaic and everyone translated them as well as he could."

It is thought that along with the many priests accepting the faith, there could also have been a number of scribes. These could well have been employed in making copies of Jesus' sayings for the new believers.

For some years after Pentecost these sayings of Jesus would have been the only written teaching that the far-flung groups of believers had as a basis for their own faith and from which they could teach others.

Modern scholars have designated these sayings of Jesus as Q, from the German word Quelle meaning source.   This Q document is thought to have provided the basis for the gospels of both Matthew and Luke where the teachings of Jesus are concerned.   Both writers then added other information they had personally gathered.

### HEBREW GOSPEL

A few years later Matthew is thought to have issued his fuller gospel,[4] written in Hebrew (or Aramaic) and directed primarily at Jewish converts.  His twice-used phrase, "to this day", would seem to indicate a date not many years removed from the event.

Matthew built around the teachings of Jesus details of his birth, life, ministry, death and resurrection. His chief aim was to show the Jews just how completely Jesus had fulfilled the Old Testament prophecies about the Messiah. The phrase, "that it might be fulfilled" appears many times in Matthew's gospel.

This Hebrew edition of Matthew was used by the Jewish and Syrian churches for many years. It was taken to India by Bartholomew, and both Jerome and Epiphanius mention it as still being in use in some places up to the fifth century.

Origen wrote, "I accept the traditional view of the four gospels... First to be written was that of the one-time exciseman who became an apostle of Jesus Christ - Matthew: it was published for believers of Jewish origin and was composed in Aramaic. Next came that of Mark who followed Peter's instructions in writing it ... Next came that of Luke, who wrote for Gentile converts. Last of all came John's."

Most scholars readily accept an early date for this Hebrew gospel of Matthew.

Schofield, in his introduction to Matthew's gospel, writes: "The date of Matthew has been much discussed, but no convincing reason has been given for discrediting the traditional date of AD 37."

Fausset writes, "Matthew's gospel answers to the first or Jewish period (of the church), ending about AD 41, and was written probably in and for Jerusalem and Judea."

Matthew Henry, Halley and other Bible scholars generally agree with an early date for this gospel. Ancient testimony is also unanimous that Matthew wrote the first gospel, and that he wrote it in Hebrew for Jewish believers.

However, the gospel according to Matthew which we have in our present Bibles is not generally believed to have been translated from this early Hebrew gospel but from a later Greek edition.

Jerome wrote, "Matthew, who is also called Levi, and who changed from a tax-gatherer into an apostle, was the first one in Judaea to write a gospel of Jesus Christ in Hebrew letters and words for those of the circumcision who believed; but who translated it afterwards into Greek is not sufficiently certain."

## GREEK GOSPEL

There seem to be three main theories regarding the origin of our present gospel of Matthew.

1.  That Matthew himself rewrote his gospel in Greek[5] some years later, adding extra material for the sake of the many new Greek-speaking converts then swelling the church. This is thought to have been around 45AD, before Matthew left Jerusalem for extended missionary service.

2.  That someone else, possibly James the Less, translated the original gospel from Aramaic into Greek.

3.  That someone other than Matthew wrote the entire Greek gospel some time after 70AD using Matthew's name to gain acceptance for their work.

Unger says : "The book of Matthew ... does not report the fall of Jerusalem and the temple but describes these events as still future. Since Luke's gospel is earlier than Acts and Matthew is certainly earlier than Luke, it seems entirely probable that if he wrote an Aramaic original he did so probably around 40-45AD.

"This would place the Greek Matthew around the middle of the first century AD.   Seventeen independent witnesses of the first four centuries attest its genuineness."

Fausset writes : "The apostle John sanctioned the gospel of Matthew as authentic. The Hebraisms suit the earliest period of the church. Early Christian writers quote the Greek not the Hebrew version with implicit confidence in its authority as Matthew's work.

"Our Greek Matthew has few, if any traces of being a translation, it has the general marks of being an independent work."

Matthew is always placed first in the canon of New Testament books. If Mark's gospel was written by 45AD, as implied by the Dead Sea Scrolls, then Matthew's Aramaic gospel must have been written earlier than this date and no doubt his Greek version followed around this time.

Origen wrote: "Of all the disciples of the Lord only Matthew and John have left us their memoirs, and they, it is reported, had recourse to writing only under the pressure of necessity, for Matthew who preached earlier to the Hebrews, when he was about to go to others also, committing his gospel in writing in his native tongue, compensated by his writing for the loss of his presence to those from whom he was sent away."

## JUDEA

Clement of Alexandria states that Matthew worked out from Jerusalem[6] for fifteen years after the resurrection, preaching mainly to the Hebrews. During this time, he tells us, Matthew preached to the Greeks of Macedonia, the Syrians and the Persians.

Ambrose connects him with Persia, Paulinus of Nola with Parthia and Isidore with Macedonia.

Eustathius says that after our Lord's ascension Matthew preached in Judaea and then in foreign nations.

So it would appear that for fifteen years after the resurrection Matthew made Jerusalem his base, with trips to Macedonia, Syria, Persia and Parthia.

During this time he also wrote the Sayings of the Lord, followed by his Hebrew gospel. Then before leaving Judaea, around 45AD, he could have written his Greek version of the Gospel bearing his name.

But where did Matthew go for his main sphere of missionary service?

## ETHIOPIA

Socrates in his Ecclesiastical History (1:19), tells us that when the apostles divided the nations between them Matthew was allotted Ethiopia[7] as his field of labour. Clement of Alexandria also says that Matthew went to the Ethiopians. This tradition has been generally accepted, even though the details remain open to discussion.

Matthew is said to have been welcomed with great honour into the home of the Ethiopian eunuch who had been baptised by Philip nearly fifteen years earlier.

Named as Judich in Ethiopian tradition, Eusebius calls him the 'first Gentile to receive the mysteries of the divine word'. He is said to have already preached the gospel in Arabia Felix and throughout Ethiopia and had brought Candace herself to the faith in the religious capital, Napata.

The Ethiopian church claims Judich as their country's first evangelist and sees his conversion as a fulfilment of Psalm 68:31 which says, "Cush (or Ethiopia) will submit herself to God." And, Zephaniah 3:10, which states, "From beyond the rivers of Cush (or Ethiopia) my worshipers ... will bring Me offerings."

The Ethiopia referred to here is not the modern country of the same name but the ancient kingdom of Meroe which lay along the upper Nile south of Aswan at the first cataract, south to Khartoum in the Sudan.

Each young king of Ethiopia was venerated as a child of the sun and was regarded as too sacred a person to administer the secular duties of state. These functions were fulfilled by a strong succession of queen mothers, each of whom was called Candace, in the same way as Egyptian rulers were titled Pharaoh.

In Old Testament times the land was called Cush (or Kush). The people were later called Nubians with the Egyptian king, Tutenkhamen being the son of a Nubian woman. The Nubians (or Ethiopians) were Semitic in language as opposed to the Abyssinians who were Hamitic.

Napata, capital of the ancient kingdom of Cush, was situated downstream from the fourth cataract of the Nile and is now in Sudan. In 295BC the royal capital was moved from Napata across the Nile to Meroe to facilitate trade with Egypt. Napata, however, remained the religious capital and royal burials continued there.

The Candaces always spoke out freely and gave strong leadership to their people. Around 24BC Egypt came under Roman control. The Romans then attempted to make Nubia pay tribute to them, leading to the first confrontation between Nubia and the Romans.

The Candace or queen mother of the time, named Amanirenas, led her armies into battle with the Romans and defeated three of their cohorts. She also defaced a statue of Emperor Augustus Caesar, bringing the head back to Nubia as a prize. This head was buried in the doorway of an important building as a final act of disrespect.

During the battle, Candace lost an eye, but this only made her more courageous. The Roman governor, Gaius Petronius, referred to her as "One-eyed Candace", but a historian of the period wrote, "This Queen had courage above her sex."

The Nubian queens, or Candaces, were also accorded a priestly role in the worship of the female goddess Isis, the main religion of Nubia. They were thus revered by their subjects as both temporal rulers and also religious leaders.

This, then, was the type of queen under whom the Ethiopian eunuch, Judich, served as treasurer.

Judich would have been a highly educated and wealthy man. He was obviously desirous of knowing the one true God, but because he was a eunuch he was prevented from becoming a full Jewish proselyte.

The grace of Christ, however, overcame all barriers and this seeking man would have been overjoyed at the message Philip brought to him. Especially so when he discovered that the God who knew the cry of his heart, had personally directed Philip to him.

Although Ethiopia had its own language, similar to Egyptian hieroglyphics, all trade and official business was transacted in Greek. Judich may also have understood Hebrew, as there were considerable Jewish settlements in Upper Egypt, just north of Aswan, and Ethiopia.

It is quite possible that both Judich and Candace had held discussions with Jewish leaders, before Judich's trip to Jerusalem.

This may have led to Judich purchasing the scroll of Isaiah, at considerable monetary cost, in the hope of finding the answers to their many questions. If so, the way could well have been prepared for Candace to accept the message of Jesus the Messiah and Saviour, upon Judich's return from Palestine.

The Apostolic History of Abdias,[8] Book VII, and several other sources gives us more details of Matthew's possible ministry both in Ethiopia and in Upper Egypt.

Soon after Matthew arrived in Ethiopia, he is said to have overcome two magicians, Zaroes and Arfaxat, who had held the people in bondage, and they fled the country. Matthew brought deliverance to the people who had been afflicted by the magicians, healed those who were sick, and baptised many in the name of the Lord.

Candace asked Matthew how he could speak in other languages and he explained to her about the Tower of Babel and the Day of Pentecost.

After Matthew had been some time in Ethiopia, word was received that Euphranor, son of the King of Upper Egypt, was dead. Candace sent word to keep him there until Matthew arrived.

When Matthew reached the palace, the queen, Euphenissa, fell at his feet. Matthew consoled her, then he raised Euphranor from the dead. He also healed his sister, the princess Ephigenia, from leprosy.

When the people knew of all this, they came to sacrifice to Matthew as a god. He restrained them, preached to them, and persuaded them to build a church instead.  It was called the Church of the Resurrection.

Matthew converted and baptised the King, Aeglippus, the queen, prince and princess who all became dedicated Christians. Matthew is said to have resided there for twenty-three years, and to have brought many to the Lord, both by his preaching and by the many miracles which he wrought.

King Aeglippus was succeeded by his brother, Hyrtacus, who wished to marry Ephigenia. He offered Matthew half his kingdom to persuade her, but Ephigenia had vowed to consecrate herself to the Lord and not to marry.  Matthew therefore refused him.

Hyrtacus was furious, and as Matthew stood at the church altar praying, a soldier sent by Hyrtacus pierced him in the back and he died. This is said to have happened on the 21st September of probably 68AD.

The people threatened to burn the palace but the Christian leaders restrained them.  Ephigenia gave all her wealth to the church. Hyrtacus was struck with a serious disease and stabbed himself to death.

Beor, the brother of Ephigenia, a Christian, succeeded Hyrtacus and reigned for twenty-five years, dying at the age of eighty-eight. He had peace with the Romans and the Persians and built many churches throughout Ethiopia and Upper Egypt.

When Jesus chose Matthew, the former tax gatherer, as one of his inner twelve, even the other disciples must have looked askance at His choice. But Jesus knew the heart of this man and he also saw the potential in Matthew's ability to write.   The debt the early church owed to this once despised outcast was enormous.

Matthew was also another of the twelve apostles to witness to a foreign king and queen. Yet it is the legacy of his meticulous gospel depicting Jesus as the promised Messiah of Israel and Saviour of the world, which will  make us forever indebted to the apostle known as Matthew-Levi.

## REFERENCES FOR MATTHEW

1.  Matthew 9:9,  Mark 2:14,  Luke 5:27-31,  8:13, Unger (Dict) pp 705-706, Barclay p 61
2.  Enc Brit Macro Vol 16 p 709, Int Std Bible Enc Vol 3   p 697,

Wenham pp 112-114, Thiede (L) pp38-42, 200, Thiede (P) pp122,129 200, Eusebius(W) p 262-263 (Origen)

3. Acts 2:8-11, 6:7, Eusebius (W) p 152, Hunter pp 25-27, 33, 34, 38, Enc Brit Micro Vol VI p 697, Thiede (P) pp 80,144,150

4. Matthew 27:7-8, 28:15, Schofield p 993, Halley p 414, Thiede (L) p41, Henry & Scott p 562, Eusebius (W) pp 213-214, 265 (Origen), G Taylor p 53, Fausset p 458 (Epiphanius 29:9), McBirnie p 175, Barclay pp 62-63, Wenham pp 112-122, 201-202, 238-243, Jerome p 362

5. Eusebius (W) p 152, Acts 2:8-11, Unger (Dict) p 706, Stonehouse pp 46-47, Fox (Z) p 3 (James the Less), Fausset pp 458-459

6. McBirnie pp 175, 181, Barclay p 63, Unger (Dict) p 705

7. McBirnie pp 175-182, 243, Eusebius (W) p 74, Hunter p 37, Fausset pp 110 (Judich, Candace), 215, 458, Unger (A:NT) pp 153-155, NIV p 1565, Enc Brit Vol VI pp 697, 809, VII, p 186, Jackson p 42, Latourette p 101, Fox (Z) p 3, (B) p 7, Barclay p 64

8. James p 466, McBirnie pp 179-180

# MATTHIAS

The first time we meet Matthias[1] is in the upper room of John Mark's home in Jerusalem. His name is thought to be a variant of Mattathias meaning 'Gift of Jehovah'.

Just before Jesus was taken up into heaven, He told his disciples to wait in Jerusalem until they were filled with the Holy Spirit. For the next ten days one hundred and twenty disciples prayed and waited expectantly.

These included the eleven apostles, the mother and brothers of Jesus and probably most of the seventy sent out by Jesus. Also present were most likely the women who had followed Jesus from Galilee, the Bethany family and others believers from the Jerusalem area.

Sometime during these ten days Peter decided they needed to elect a replacement for Judas to keep the number of apostles to twelve. Quoting a verse from the Psalms which declared, "May another take his place of leadership", Peter suggested they appoint two men from among their number and draw lots for God to show them which one He wanted.

To qualify, the men must have been with them "the whole time the Lord Jesus went in and out among us, beginning from John's baptism to the time when Jesus was taken up from us. For one of these must become a witness with us of his resurrection."

The two men chosen were Joseph called Barsabbas (also known as Justus) and Matthias. 'Then they prayed, "Lord, you know everyone's heart. Show us which of these two you have chosen to take over this apostolic ministry." They cast lots and the lot fell to Matthias, so he was added to the eleven apostles.'

To have been present at the baptism of Jesus, it is thought that the two men must have previously been disciples of John the Baptist.

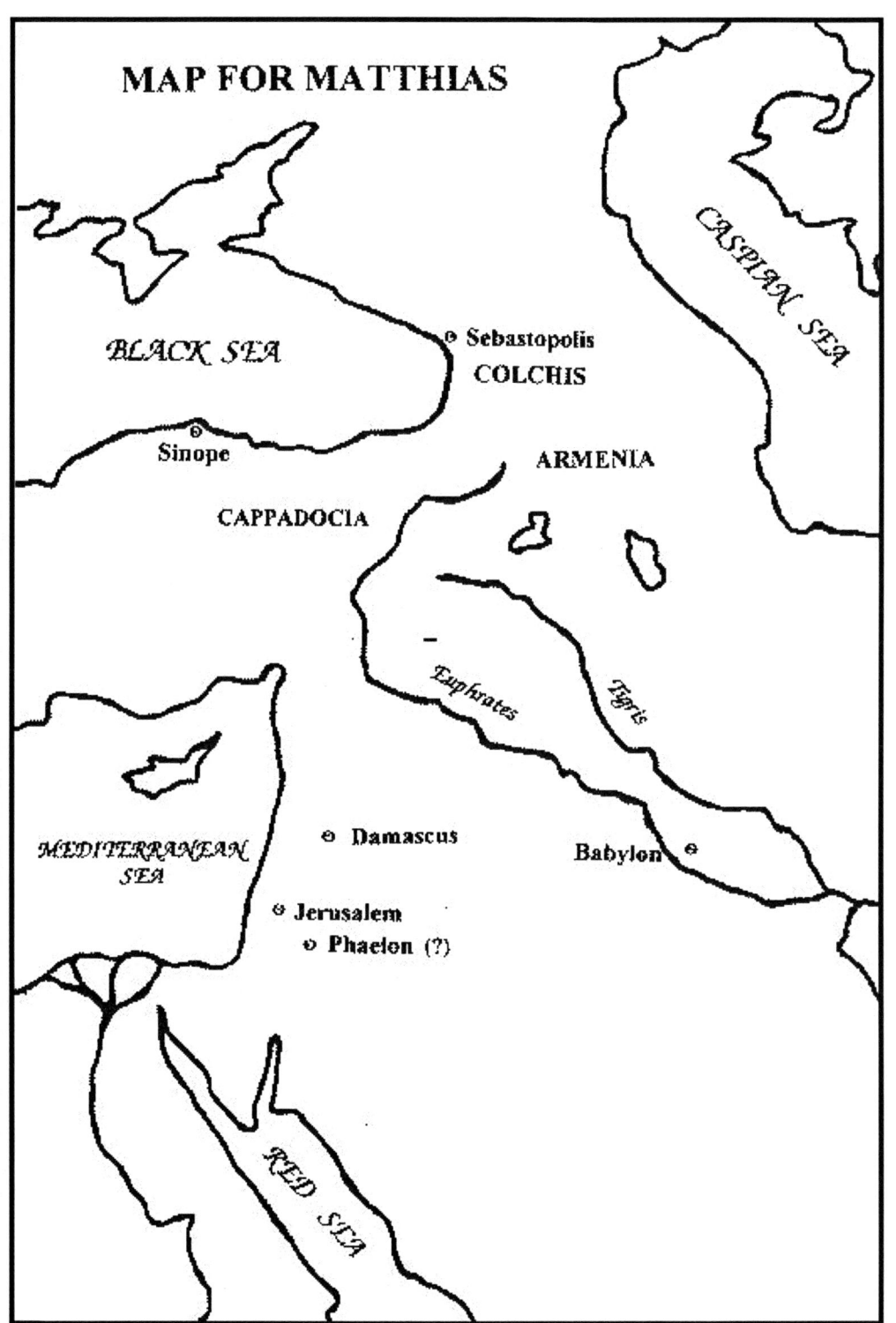

# MAP FOR MATTHIAS

CASPIAN SEA

BLACK SEA

⊙ Sebastopolis
COLCHIS

⊙ Sinope

ARMENIA

CAPPADOCIA

Euphrates

Tigris

MEDITERRANEAN
SEA

⊙ Damascus

Babylon ⊙

⊙ Jerusalem
⊙ Phaelon (?)

RED SEA

Eusebius states that both men were members of the seventy. Jerome, Clement and Epiphanius all mention that Matthias was one of the seventy.[2] In this role the two men must have shown qualities of dedication and leadership which had greatly impressed the apostles.

When the Holy Spirit fell on the gathered disciples on the Day of Pentecost, Matthias would have received a special enduement of power along with the others. He would also have been involved in teaching and instructing the new believers.

Clement of Alexandria, in his writings, quotes from the Traditions of Matthias. He states that Matthias was remarkable for teaching the necessity of mortifying the flesh with its irregular passions and desires.[3]

Matthias is said to have ministered in Judea for a time, then to have travelled to the mountainous country of Cappadocia[4] where he spent some time preaching the gospel.

From there he is said to have travelled to Armenia.[5] The Armenian church credits him with being one of five apostles to have evangelised their country. The others were Jude Thaddaeus, Bartholomew, Simon the Zealot and Andrew.

During his time in this area, Matthias is said to have suffered imprisonment and other perils at Sebastopol and Colchis. Some accounts consider he met his martyrdom at Colchis.

However, the apocryphal Acts of Andrew and Matthias[6] tells how the apostles divided the countries of the world among themselves. Then follows an extremely imaginative account of the Lord directing Andrew to go and rescue Matthias from the land of the cannibals.

While the details are rather preposterous, it is nevertheless possible that Andrew may have helped to rescue Matthias there at one time. The two may then have worked together in the area around Sebastopol and Colchis for a while before Matthias moved back to Judea.

The Martyrdom[7] of St Matthias states that he was sent to Damascus, and later died at Phaleaon, a city of Judea. Other sources mention Jerusalem as the place of Matthias's ministry and burial. The tradition is that he was stoned to death there by the Jews.

It would seem that after surviving the perils of missionary service in foreign lands, Matthias returned to Jerusalem, possibly anticipating a respite from his sufferings, only to be martyred by his own countrymen.

The date given for his death is 64AD and the day on which he is remembered is the 24th February, which may also be the date of his martyrdom.

His body is said to have been kept at Jerusalem for about three hundred years, after which St Helena, mother of the Emperor Constantine, had it taken to Rome.

Thus the twelfth apostle, although late in being 'ordained' as Irenaeus states, nevertheless served his Lord faithfully unto death. If his name is among those on the foundations of the New Jerusalem, it would seem the honour was well  and truly earned.

## REFERENCES FOR MATTHIAS

1. Acts 1:12-26, Psalm 109:8, Unger (Dict) p 706
2. Luke 10:1-24, Eusebius (W) pp 64, 71, McBirnie p 242, Fausset p 460 (Epiphanius 1:20), Enc Brit Vol VI p 698,
3. Unger (Dict) p 706, McBirnie pp 242, 243
4. Enc Brit Vol VI p 698
5. McBirnie pp 207, 243,
6. McBirnie p 245, James pp 453-458
7. McBirnie pp 242, 244, 245

# PETER

In the gospels Peter[1] always seems to be in the forefront of any action, whether it be walking on the water, making profound spiritual statements or swearing profanely as he denies even knowing Jesus. When Jesus first met Peter He told him that although his name was Simon, it was going to become Cephas or Peter, both of which mean rock.

Throughout the gospels kindhearted, sanguine Simon was nevertheless often impulsive, zealous, outspoken and as changeable as shifting sand. Yet in spite of all this, Jesus saw in him the potential of a great leader.

Peter and his younger brother Andrew were the sons of John, and according to tradition their mother was Johanna.

Peter was married and had a mother-in-law who lived with them. Clement of Alexandria states that Peter had a family, and Alford adds that he had a son and daughter, named elsewhere as Petronilla.

In Paul's letter to the Corinthians he says Peter's wife, whom Clement names as Perpetua, went with him on his ministry trips. Clement adds that the wives of both Peter and Philip travelled with them and "helped them in ministering to women at their homes, and by them the doctrine of the Lord penetrated, without scandal, into the privacy of the women's apartments."

## LEADER

From early on Peter seems to have been generally accepted as leader[2] or spokesman for the twelve, and on several occasions he did in fact receive special commissions from Jesus.

In the upper room it was Peter who decided that they should elect another apostle to take the place of Judas Iscariot.

Then on the Day of Pentecost Peter automatically took the lead, preaching to the multitude and winning three thousand people to the Lord with one sermon.

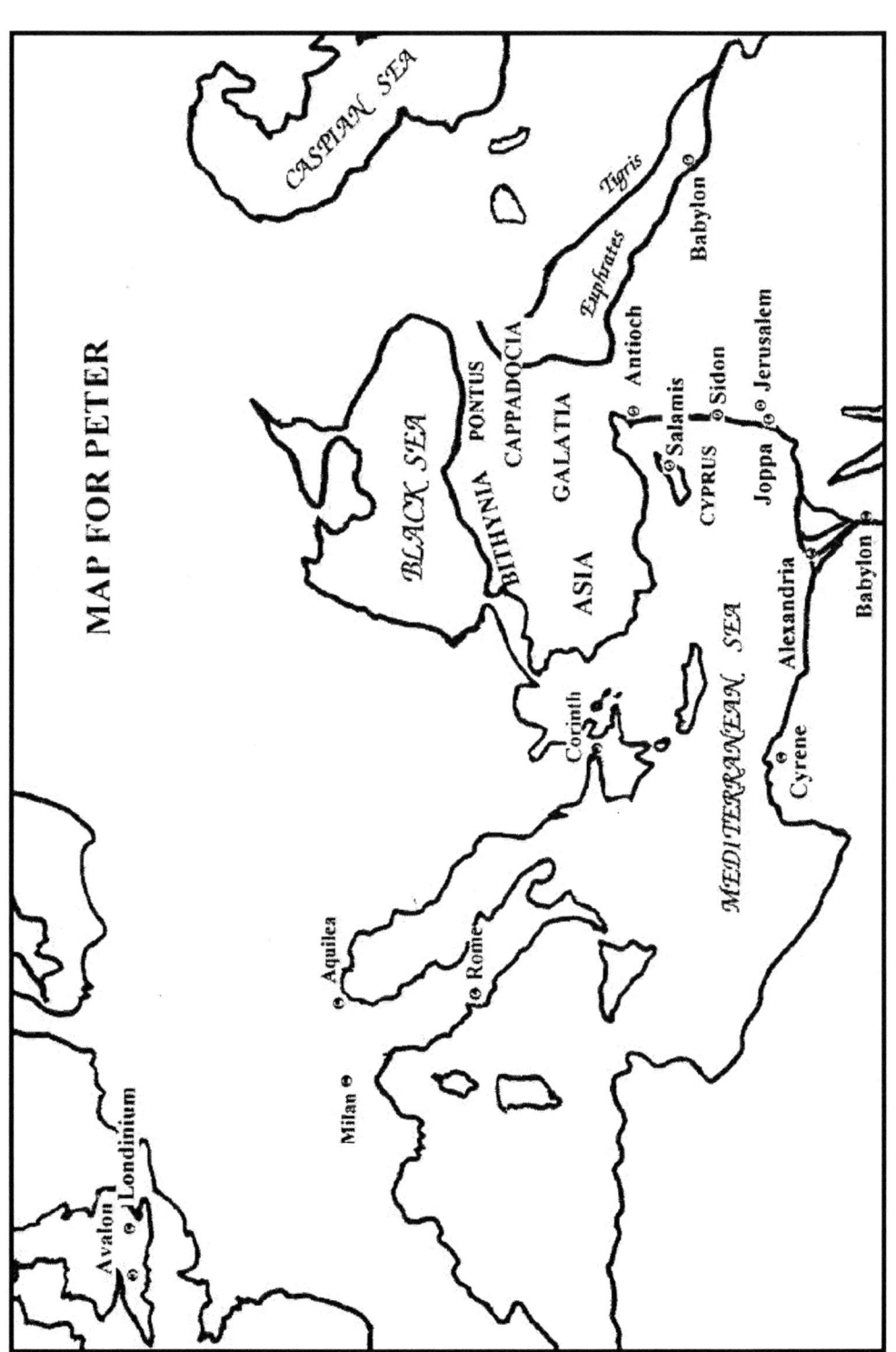

MAP FOR PETER

From then on his days were full.  Between preaching daily in Solomon's Collonade, praying for the sick and spending time in prison, Peter certainly  seems to have headed up the work of establishing the young church.

During this time John appears to have been Peter's constant companion, even to sharing imprisonment with him.  Yet in healing the lame man at the Gate Beautiful, witnessing fearlessly to the high priest, or dealing with Ananias and Sapphira, Peter was the one through whom the Holy Spirit spoke with authority.

Luke tells us that crowds gathered from the towns around Jerusalem, bringing their sick and those tormented by evil spirits and all of them were healed. As a result, people brought their sick into the streets and laid them on mats so that at least Peter's shadow might fall on them as he passed by.

This was a tremendous responsibility for a basically unschooled fisherman from Galilee. But the three years Peter had spent with Jesus, the humbling effect of his betrayal of his Lord, followed by the dramatic infilling of the Holy Spirit had all worked towards transforming unstable Simon into Peter the rock.

## EARLY MINISTRY

Not long after Pentecost, Eusebius tells us, Peter, James and John appointed James the brother of Jesus as head of the Jerusalem church, freeing themselves and the other apostles to engage in evangelistic work elsewhere.[3]

From mid-32AD to April 44AD Peter seems to have interspersed his ministry at Jerusalem with trips to various centres in Palestine, and possibly some even further afield.

In Acts we read of his early ministry in Samaria, probably around 32AD, then around 38AD, we read of his extensive ministry in the towns on the Plain of Sharon. Highlights of this time were the healing of the paralytic, Aeneas, at Lydda and the raising of Dorcas from the dead at Joppa, followed by the conversion of Cornelieus and his household at Caesarea.

However, except for Paul's visit to Jerusalem around 35AD, when he spent fifteen days with Peter, we don't have any further details of Peter's ministry in the years up to 44AD.

Tradition states that Peter paid a visit to Phoenecia early in his ministry. Luke tells us in Acts that in the persecution that followed the stoning of Stephen, those who were scattered abroad went as far as Phoenecia, Cyprus and Antioch, sharing the good news of Christ.

Jesus visited Tyre and Sidon at least once, and we read in the gospels that many people from that area came to Galilee to hear Jesus preach and to be healed. Therefore it is quite probable that Peter did visit Phoenecia during this time, to confirm the work as he had in Samaria.

On his way there Peter no doubt visited the believers who are said to have met regularly in Peter's own house in Capernaum. Archaeologists claim to have found the ruins of Peter's house under a fourth century church carefully erected over the site.

Antioch and Babylon also claim Peter as one of their early founders. It is quite possible that Peter did indeed visit either or both of these important Jewish centres early on where he would have preached to the "Jews only". It was after men from Cyprus and Cyrene preached the gospel to the Greeks in Antioch, around 41AD, that the Jerusalem church sent Barnabas to check things out.

The Church of the East, originating in Babylon, claims to have been founded by the apostles Peter, Thomas, Jude Thaddaeus and Mari of the Seventy. As Thomas probably reached Babylon in late 32AD, if Peter did preach there early on it would most likely have been late 33-34AD or sometime after Paul's visit to Jerusalem in 35AD.

## ANOTHER PLACE

In April 44AD, following the beheading of James by Herod Agrippa I and Peter's own miraculous escape from prison, we are told in Acts that Peter left Jerusalem for 'another place'[4]. There has been much speculation as to where this could have been. It would certainly have been somewhere outside of Herod's jurisdiction.

Matthew Henry says, "Hales considers Peter went to Antioch, while Townsend considers that he went to Rome." Yet others feel he may have gone to Babylon at this time.

If Peter was at Antioch in 44AD, it seems surprising that there is no mention of him when Paul, Barnabas and John Mark returned from Jerusalem a short time later. Neither was he included in the prayer group which commissioned Paul and Barnabas for their missionary work soon after.

Also, if The Apostolic History of Abdias is correct, then Jude Thaddaeus and Simon the Zealot would have been active in Babylon during 44-45AD, and there is no mention in early writings of Peter being there at that time.

## ROME

Both Eusebius and Jerome, however, state that Peter went to Rome[5] around this time. To counter claims of Peter's supremacy by the Roman Catholic church, Protestant writers have often tried to establish that Peter was never in Rome before the time of his death in 67AD. Yet there are quite a number of references stating that he was there at least once and probably twice before this time.

Scholars such as Jackson, Thiede, Robinson, Wenham and others hold to the view that Peter did indeed go to Rome after his escape from Herod.

Eusebius, quoting Irenaeus and Justin Martyr, relates that Simon Magus, after being rebuked by Peter in Samaria, went on to Rome to continue his occult practices. But, he continues, in the reign of Claudius (41-54AD), Peter arrived to again withstand Simon's evil ways. Hippolytus also mentions the contest between Simon Magus and Peter.

Dionysius, bishop of Corinth, in a letter to Soter in Rome, 170AD, writes that both Corinth and Rome were founded by Peter and Paul, and that both were martyred at the same time. In his foot note in Eusebius p 107, the translator, G A Williamson states, "Both Dionysius and Irenaeus put Peter before Paul as they believed his arrival in Rome to be prior to Paul's, as did Eusebius."

Although there were apparently a great number of Christians in Rome by 44AD, it would seem that Peter was the first apostle to preach there, and is therefore classed as its founder.

## MARK

Eusebius tells us that not long after Peter's arrival he was joined by Mark[6], who, having a knowledge of Latin and Roman ways, acted as Peter's interpreter.

Atiya and others state that Mark came from a wealthy Cyrenian family. He was highly intelligent, being fluent in Hebrew, Aramaic, Greek, Latin and possibly even Egyptian. Mark and his mother, Mary, are said to have moved to Jerusalem on the death of Mark's father, not long before the crucifixion.

In Jerusalem they bought a large house with an upper room that could accommodate one hundred and twenty people. They also had at least two servants, the man with the water pot and Rhoda.

Mark had set out with Paul and Barnabas on their missionary trip in 44AD. Being used to having servants of his own, however, Mark apparently had difficulty accepting his menial role as servant to the somewhat overbearing Paul. Before long he left them and returned to Jerusalem.

Here he learned that Herod Agrippa had died in early August. Immediately he set out for Rome to tell Peter the good news.

There seems to have been a special bond between Peter and Mark. In Mark's gospel we read of a young man running naked from the scene of Jesus' arrest. Townson and others consider this to have been Mark himself, as no-one else mentions it. Roused from sleep by Judas and the soldiers seeking Jesus at his home, Mark, who was probably about seventeen at the time, wrapped his linen sheet around him and followed at a distance. When one of the soldiers in Gethsemane grabbed at his linen cloth, Mark pulled free and made good his escape.

Mark would no doubt have heard the various reports of Jesus' resurrection appearances, some of them in the upper room of his own home.

Then on the Day of Pentecost he would almost certainly have witnessed the amazing events which unfolded with the outpouring of the Holy Spirit in that same upper room.

Soon after, we are told, Mark was won to the Lord and baptised by Peter himself. In seeming confirmation of this, at the close of Peter's first episistle he refers to Mark as his 'son'.

. It is thought that Mark may have been one of the 'believers' who accompanied Peter on his preaching trips to places like Joppa and Caesarea during the fourteen years he worked out from Jerusalem. Otherwise it is difficult to imagine that Mark could have recorded Peter's words so accurately in his gospel after just a few months of working together with him in Rome.

## PUDENS

Cardinal Baronius[7] tells us that "Rufus the Senator received St Peter into his house on Viminalis Hill in the year 44AD." In his letter to Timothy some years later, Paul writes, "Eubulus greets you, as well as Pudens, Linus, Claudia and all the brethren."

The Pudens mentioned by Paul is believed to have been Rufus Pudens, son of the above-mentioned Senator. At the time of Peter's first visit to Rome, Pudens junior was away in Britain serving under General Aulus Plautius in the Claudian-Caradoc war.

There were many Christians in Rome from soon after Pentecost, and the Senator seems to have been one of the early converts. His son, however, was still a pagan. Pudens junior was in command of the regiment at Regnum, the name for the Roman encampment at Chichester.

In 1723AD workmen excavated a large marble plaque at Chichester with a citation dedicating a temple to Neptune and Minerva. The site, it says, was given by Pudens, son of Pudentinus.

The temple was erected about 50AD, two years before the return of Pudens to Rome.

It may well be that the senior Pudens encouraged Peter to take his life-changing message to those, including his son, in the extreme west of the then-known world.

## BRITAIN

In Acts there is no mention of Peter between his leaving for 'another place' in 44AD and his attendance at the church council of late 49AD. Also, apart from the Roman Catholic church's claim of Peter's twenty-five year residency at Rome, there are no other accounts of his ministry during this time.

However, although the evidence is not very strong, there are a number of traditions stating that Peter did go to Britain at this time.[8] As McBirnie states, "There certainly is no reason why Peter could not have visited Great Britain. Many believe he did."

Jowett quotes Cornelius a Lapide as stating, "Peter ... was absent in Britain." And Simon Metaphrastes quotes Eusebius as saying, "St Peter to have been in Britain as well as in Rome."

Eusebius in his De Demonstratione Evangelii, lib.iii, wrote, "The apostles passed beyond the ocean to the isles called the Britannic Isles."

In recent times an ancient, rough-hewn stone monument was excavated at Whithorn, near a Celtic Christian settlement.   On its face was an inscription reading, "The Place of St Peter the Apostle."

According to Jowett Peter made his base at Avalon - present-day Glastonbury - where Joseph of Arimathea and his band had been ministering for eight years.   Peter would no doubt have worked with Joseph and his band for a while before proceeding further afield.

A wattle and daub church measuring twenty meters long by eight meters wide had been completed early in 39AD.   This is thought to have been the first Christian church erected anywhere in the world.

The building was so revered that  it was later encased in lead. Then in 630AD Paulinus erected over it the chapel of St Marys which remained intact until 1184AD when fire gutted the whole Abbey.   Today only its ruins remain as mute testimony to those early missionaries to Britain.

Jowett, Morgan and others state that among the early converts of Joseph and his group were members of the Royal Silurian household. One of these was Arviragus, Duke of Cornwall, who is said to have welcomed Joseph and his group warmly and to have given them a grant of twelve hides of land.   This land is recorded in the Doomsday book as being free from tax for ever.

Arviragus' cousin was King Caradoc of the Welsh Silures. He was to become famous in Roman history books as Caractacus,  the man who, for nine years of almost continuous warfare, repelled the might of the Roman army. Caradoc's sister, Gladys, his elder daughter, Eurgain, and his son Linus, who later became the first bishop of Rome, were all said to be among Joseph's early converts.

This is the group which Peter is thought to have  joined at Avalon early in 45AD.   At the time war was raging in the east of Britain between the British warriors under Caradoc and the  Roman troops under General Aulus Plautius.

The Greek historian, Dio Cassius, gives a vivid account of the fighting between the two sides. Eventually Aulus Plautius sent word to Rome for reinforcements. Claudius responded by arriving in Britain with a group of elephants to intimidate the foe.   Caradoc's horses were terrified by the odour of these unknown animals and immediately scattered in all directions.

This led to Caradoc's defeat at Brandon Camp on the Teme.

Claudius effected a treaty, known as the Claudian Treaty, and offered his daughter, Venus Julia, called in the British accounts Venissa, in marriage to Arviragus. The marriage took place in later years.

Both Suetonius and Dio Cassius state that Claudius was back in Rome within six months to celebrate a great triumph, albeit a little prematurely, for his conquest of Britain.

During the period of truce, Jowett and others state that General Aulus Plautius, no doubt thinking the war was over, wooed and won the hand of the beautiful and talented sister of Caradoc, princess Gladys, later named Pomponia Graecina by the Romans.

At the wedding was Rufus Pudens, son of the Roman senator. He seems to have been attracted to the younger daughter of Caradoc, named Gladys after her aunt, who was then a fair-haired, blue-eyed lass of about nine.

It may also have been during this period of truce that Peter preached in London at a place known as Cornhill.[9]   In 179 AD the first Christian church in London was erected on this spot by King Lucius, a descendant of Arviragus. It was dedicated to the memory of St Peter in commemoration of his evangelising labours in Britain. Named St Peter's on Cornhill, it was partially destroyed during the great fire of London, but the plaque relating the history of the church was saved and now stands over the mantle of the fireplace in the vestry of the rebuilt church.

At the conclusion of the truce period, however, hostilities resumed almost immediately between the two sides and preaching was once again confined to the west of the country around Cornwall, Somerset and Wales.

Aulus Plautius was appointed governor of Britain, but because of the difficulties involved in having to fight his brother-in-law, Plautius was eventually recalled to Rome in 47AD and General Ostorius Scapula took his place.

Tacitus tells us that in 57AD "Pomponia Graecina, a woman of illustrious birth, and the wife of Aulus Plautius, who, on his return from Britain, entered the city with the pomp of an ovation, was accused of embracing the rites of a foreign superstition.

The matter was referred to the jurisdiction of her husband. Plautius, in conformity to ancient usage, called together a number of her relations, and in her presence, sat in judgement on the conduct of his wife. He pronounced her innocent."

Plautius would have known his wife was a Christian when he married her, and he was at least sympathetic to Christianity at this stage. Some time later he also became a Christian.

If the foregoing details regarding Peter are correct, then it would seem he may have spent almost four years in Britain, returning to Rome in the spring of 49AD. Here, both Eusebius and Jerome tells us, Peter was met by Philo,[10] the Jewish philosopher from Alexandria, who wanted to talk with him about Mark and the church he had established in that city. Jerome adds that Philo enjoyed Peter's friendship. Philo is said to have died about 50AD, at the age of seventy, so his visit to Peter could not have been any later than this.

## MARK'S GOSPEL

Peter had probably left Rome for Britain soon after the shipping lanes reopened from the winter shut-down on the 10th March, 45AD. We read in Eusebius that after his 'departure', the people begged Mark to put into writing the things Peter had told them. That Mark did so, while most likely staying at the Pudens' mansion, is recorded four times in Eusebius, quoting Papias, Irenaeus, Clement and Origen. The only point in dispute is the date of writing.

Some scholars have decided that Peter's 'departure' meant his death, and have therefore dated Mark's gospel[11] around 67AD or later.

Bruce, Wenham and others, however, consider that the word 'excessio' used for 'departure' means exodus or leaving, not death.

Clement of Alexandria and Papias both relate that when Peter heard about Mark's gospel, he was delighted and authorised the reading of it in all the churches.

As further backing for an early date to Mark's gospel, nineteen fragments of papyrus found among the Dead Sea Scrolls discovered at Qmran in 1947, have been dated at around 50AD. For the Essenes to have possessed a copy of Mark's gospel at this early date, it must have been in circulation for several years prior to them obtaining a copy.

The History of the Patriarchs mentions that the revelation to Peter and Mark that Mark should take the gospel to Alexandria,[12] came in the fifteenth year after the Ascension of Christ, or 45AD.

Eusebius, Atiya and other writers state that after completing his gospel, Mark departed for Cyrene, his original home town, taking a copy of his gospel with him. After spending some time "performing many miracles, sowing the seeds of his faith" and generally encouraging the believers at Cyrene, Mark then left to take his gospel into Egypt.

Atiya tells us that Mark went by a circuitous route through the oases and Egyptian Babylon - where Simon the Zealot had preached the gospel some twelve years earlier.

On entering Alexandria by the eastern gate, which led into the Jewish quarter, Mark broke the strap of his shoe. So he sought out a cobbler to mend it. When the cobbler took an awl to work on the shoe, he accidentally pierced his hand and cried aloud, "Heis ho Theos" (God is one). Mark rejoiced at this and after miraculously healing the man's wound, preached Christ to his first convert.

The man's name was Anianus. He took Mark home with him and after Mark shared the gospel with his family all believed and were baptised. Many others soon followed, with Mark working out from the cobbler's home, and having Anianus as his assistant.

During his time in Alexandria it would seem Mark also preached to the native Egyptians. The Coptic church claims that although the Greek gospel would have sufficed, Mark had another version prepared in the Egyptian language for native converts who were not readily conversant with Greek.

So successful was Mark's ministry, however, and so strong was the church he built up there, that eventually word spread that a Galilean was in the city preparing to overthrow the idols. Popular feeling began to rise against him.

Hearing that he was being sought, Eusebius and others tell us, Mark ordained Anianus as bishop, a position he filled for twenty-two years, along with three elders and seven deacons to assist him in watching over the congregation in case anything befell Mark.

We don't know how long Mark was able to minister in Alexandria before he had to flee to Jerusalem. It may have been almost four years, but the strong work he established was so impressive that Philo visited Rome to discuss it with Peter.

The edict of Claudius in 49AD,[13] banning all Jews from Rome, and said by Suetonius to have been caused by riots over one Chrestus (Christ), saw Peter moving back to Jerusalem in time for the council of late 49AD. Here the matter of whether Gentile Christians should keep the law of Moses and be circumcised was soundly discussed, with Peter adding his testimony regarding the conversion of Cornelius and his household some years earlier.

## ANTIOCH

Following the Jerusalem council, Paul, Barnabas and John Mark, together with Silas and Judas Barsabas returned to Antioch[14] early in 50AD, to report on the outcome.

Peter apparently followed a few months later, and it may have been at this time that Paul 'withstood Peter to his face' for refusing to eat with the Gentile Christians.

Soon after this Paul suggested to Barnabas that they should revisit the towns of their earlier missionary trip to encourage and confirm the Christians in their faith. Barnabas wanted to take Mark with them, but Paul refused.

The contention was so great between them, that the two veteran missionaries parted company. Paul took Silas as his companion, and Barnabas took Mark and returned to his home-town of Salamis on the island of Cyprus.

Peter seems to have remained at Antioch for the next seven years, from 51- 58AD. Gregory the Great, Atiya and others state that Peter was the first Bishop of Antioch, and the fact of his seven-year bishopric is not generally disputed, but the date is.

Jerome gives the years as 33-40AD, with Peter then going to Rome where he is said to have served as bishop for the next twenty-five years. However, these dates do not fit in with scripture, whereas the later date allows for all other factors to be accommodated.

For instance, it is from Antioch that Peter is said to have visited Corinth, Pontus and Bithynia. Peter's visit to Corinth had to be after Paul's first visit there in 51-52AD but before the writing of Paul's first epistle to them in about 55AD. In it Paul takes the Corinthians to task for claiming that some were 'of Paul' some were 'of Apollos' and others were 'of Cephas' or Peter.

Towards the end of 58AD Peter was apparently joined by both Silas and Mark at Antioch. It is believed that Silas was one of those who accompanied Paul on his last trip to Jerusalem where he was arrested in June 58AD and taken as prisoner to Caesarea.

## MARK AND BARNABAS

Mark arrived soon after, probably seeking comfort from his 'father in Christ'.

After leaving Antioch in 50AD, Mark and Barnabas[15] had spent almost eight years serving the Lord from the island of Cyprus. They worked out from Barnabas' hometown of Salamis, apparently visiting other places, including Milan, during this time.

However, in 58AD, Elymas Bar Jesus, the Jewish astrologer whom Paul had made blind, finally saw his chance to get even. Rousing the Jews of Salamis against Barnabas, they rushed him to the hippodrome where he was brutally stoned to death.

That night Mark secretly stole the body of his cousin and buried it outside the city, under a carob tree, in an empty Roman tomb hewn from the rocky hillside. He folded Barnabas' hands across his breast over a copy of Matthew's gospel in Barnabas' own handwriting.

Barnabas is said to have died on the 11th June, 58AD, at around sixty years of age. A small chapel has been built over his tomb and can be seen in Salamis to this day.

With the arrival of Silas and Mark, Peter ordained Euodius as the second bishop of Antioch. Euodius' successor was Ignatius, whose letters, written in 107AD on his way to martyrdom in Rome, are well known.

## BABYLON

Leaving Antioch, Peter, Silas and Mark, accompanied by Peter's wife, Perpetua, then set out for Babylon on the Euphrates.[16]

After ministering to the believers there for some time, Peter apparently received news of the difficulties the Christians were experiencing in Asia. With Silas as his scribe, Peter addressed his first epistle to the Jewish Christians scattered throughout Pontus, Galatia, Cappadocia, Asia and Bithynia. He encouraged them to stand firm in their faith in spite of the many trials they were suffering.

Peter closes his epistle by mentioning Silvanus or Silas, a faithful brother to them, as the writer. He then sends greetings from his 'son' Mark, and also from 'she who is at Babylon, who is chosen together with you.'Some think Peter is referring to the church at Babylon while others consider this means his wife.

The date of Peter's first epistle has generally been thought to be around 65AD, but a number of factors would seem to indicate a slightly earlier date. Also, a complication in establishing the sequence of events for the next few years in Peter's ministry is that some writers have considered Peter was actually in Rome when he wrote his epistle, and just used Babylon as a euphemism to avoid further trouble.

Unger, Fausset, Alford and others, however, consider that a friendly letter is not the place to use 'code language' as John did in Revelation.

Fausset writes, "Babylon, a chief seat of the dispersed Jews, was his headquarters when he wrote I Peter, not Rome as some have argued. The mixture of Hebrew and Nabathaean spoken there was akin to his Galilean dialect. The well known progress that Christianity made in that quarter, as shown by the great Christian schools at Edessa and Nisibis, was probably due to Peter originally.

"The order in which Peter enumerates the countries from NE to S and W is such as one writing from Babylon would adopt."

McBirnie adds, "The traditions of the eastern-most churches are unanimous that it (I Peter) was written in Babylon, which is exactly what it says in the epistle."

If Peter had gone directly to Rome from Antioch in 58AD, it would be surprising, with Paul there from 61-63AD, that neither apostle sent greetings from the other in their respective epistles. Also, with so many Christians walking many kilometers to welcome Paul on his arrival at Puteoli, it would put Peter in a bad light if he did not so much as greet him.

If we accept that Peter did indeed write his first epistle from Babylon on the Euphrates somewhere around 62AD, we are able to slot in most of the events mentioned by various writers.

Silas was to deliver Peter's epistle to the churches in Asia as soon as it was written. Thus we find Peter, Mark and Perpetua most likely arriving in Rome early in 63AD.

## ROME

Paul, who refers to himself as an old man in his letter to Philemon, was still under house arrest in Rome.[17] In his epistle to the Colossians, written early in 63AD, he mentions Mark as being among those who are with him. In the spring of 63AD, Paul was finally set free.

The Roman Martyrologies and other accounts tell us that both Peter and Paul stayed at the British Palace and that the four children of Claudia and Pudens were taught at their knees. This seems to be the only time the two apostles could have spent time together in Rome but the exact duration is difficult to ascertain.

Second century mosaics and pictures of Peter in his latter years portray a large, well-built man with a strong face, a shock of white hair and a full white beard. Paul is shown as a smaller man with a balding forehead and a short, pointed beard.

## CARADOC

But how did the two ageing apostles come to be staying at the British Palace? The British Pendragon, Caradoc[18] and his cousin Arviragus had waged a magnificent battle against the Romans for nine long years. In the autumn of 52AD, however, Caradoc was finally betrayed by Cartimandu, queen of the Iceni, to whom he had gone for help.

The British king and his entire family were taken in chains to Rome. According to the British Triads, these included Caradoc's ninety-year-old grandfather, Llyr (Shakespear's King Lear) who died not long after his arrival in Rome. Caradoc's father, Bran the Blessed, who had resigned as king of the Silures in 36AD in favour of Caradoc to become an Arch Druid was also taken, along with Caradoc's wife, his three sons, Cyllinus, Linus and Cynon, and two daughters Eurgain and Gladys.

Tacitus tells us that more than three million people lined the streets to catch a glimpse of this famous British king who had defied Rome's greatest generals for more than nine years.

At his trial, Caradoc, or Caractacus as the Romans called him, made such an impressive speech in his own defence that, in an entirely unprecedented move, Claudius pardoned the whole family. The conditions were that most of the family remain in Rome for seven years as hostages, and that on their return to Britain, they promise never to raise arms against Rome again.

Two of Caradoc's sons, Cyllinus and Cynon were allowed to return to Britain to manage the family estates and forward revenue towards the upkeep of the family in Rome.

Linus, the middle son, remained in Rome and was eventually consecrated as the first bishop of the Roman church.

The magnificent home of the British Royal Family in Rome became known as the "British Palace." With the conversion of the whole family, this became the first Christian church building in Rome, and can still be seen to this day. Hermas, mentioned by Paul in his letter to the Romans, is said to have been their first pastor.

Sixteen-year-old Gladys had refused to leave her father's side throughout his trial. The courage and bearing of this fair-haired, blue-eyed British beauty so impressed the Emperor Claudius that he adopted her as his protege, renaming her Claudia.

Rufus Pudens, who had returned to Rome with the prisoners, had apparently not forgotten the young princess either, and in 53AD they were married.

The poet Martial wrote an epigram for his friend, Pudens, to mark the event. It read: "Although Claudia Rufina may be a blue-eyed Briton born, how much has she the disposition of the Latin race! What a graceful figure! The Italian matrons might believe her a Roman, those of Attica of their country. The gods bless her in that she proves fruitful to her pious husband."

He wrote another on the occasion of the birth of their third child, Pudentiana, four years later. The four children of Pudens and Claudia, Timotheus, (named after Timothy, to whom they sent greetings through Paul), two daughters, Pudentiana and Praxedes, and youngest son Novatus, are those said to have been brought up at the knees of Peter and Paul.

Cardinal Baronius states that "Timotheus was a son of the most noble Roman Senator, Rufus Pudens, a disciple of Sts Peter and Paul"

When H V Morton visited the Church of St Pudentiana in Rome, he was shown down into the crypt under the church where the extensive foundations and walls of a first-century Roman house were evident. He writes, "It was always the tradition that the church above occupied the site of the house of a Roman Christian called Pudens, who had entertained St Peter and St Paul, and was the Pudens mentioned in St Paul's second letter to Timothy. In 1870, men digging under the church broke their way into this Roman building.

"Some believe that he was the same Pudens to whom the poet

Martial wrote an epigram on the occasion of his marriage to a British princess who changed her name to Claudia.   Both Claudia and Pudens are mentioned by Paul in his letter to Timothy.

"If the Claudia and Pudens of Paul's letter are the Claudia and Pudens of Martial's epigram, if Pomponia Graecina, wife of Aulus Plautius, who had commanded the Roman forces in Britain, was, as many think, a Briton and a Christian, then we can indulge in the pleasing reflection that among the members of the Christian community in Rome who knew St Peter and St Paul were some natives of these islands."

## ARISTOBULUS

When Paul sends greeting to various parties at the end of his epistle to the Romans, he mentions the household  of Aristobulus.[19] The reason he doesn't greet Aristobulus himself is that a few months earlier Aristobulus,  brother of Barnabas, and one of the seventy,  is said to have accompanied the father of Caradoc, Bran the Blessed, along with other members of the family back to Britain.

Here he worked with Joseph of Arimathea for a time before moving farther afield to preach the gospel.

While Aristobulus remained under the protection of the Silures, he had complete freedom to share the message of Christ.  However, while preaching in Montgomeryshsire, Aristobulus was captured by the war-like Ordivices and martyred.

## PETER AND PAUL

Caradoc seems to have remained in Rome beyond his seven years, as the records state that he was baptised by Paul.[20]

As well as those mentioned in Paul's letter to the Romans, a man named Paron is also said to have put his house and garden, which could hold five hundred persons, at Peter's disposal for Christian gatherings.  Thus the work in Rome seems to have reached into all strata of society, with many thousands professing faith in Christ.

Tacitus tells us that following the great fire of Rome in July 64AD, thousands of Christians were martyred for their faith. Clement of Rome states that "a great multitude" perished at this time. However, there were apparently still many thousands more who survived to carry on the work. This gives us some idea of the number of

Christians in Rome around 63AD.

Paul is thought to have left Rome late in 63AD, bound for Spain, as he'd originally planned, and possibly even Britain. Clement of Rome, writing around 96AD, says Paul, "after he had been in the extremity of the west, suffered martyrdom before the sovereigns of mankind."

Theodoret, in AD 435 wrote, "Paul, liberated from his first captivity at Rome, preached the gospel to the Britons and others in the West."

On his return he was arrested in the spring of 66AD at Nicomedia or Troas, and imprisoned, either in the infamous Mamertine prison, or another prison reserved for Roman citizens.

Peter is considered to have been absent from Rome at the time of the great fire, and some feel that he also paid another visit to Britain around this time before returning to Rome in 66 AD.  It is at this time that Peter is thought to have written his second epistle to the same group of Christians as before.   Peter knew that his time was short, "as our Lord Jesus Christ has made clear to me", but seemingly he had not yet been arrested.

With Paul now in prison, however, Hegesippus tells us the Christians persuaded Peter to flee Rome.  Both Origen and Ambrose relate that as Peter left the outskirts of the city, suddenly the Lord appeared to him.

"Where are you going, Lord?" Peter asked him. Jesus replied, "I am going to Rome to be crucified again."  At this Peter felt very ashamed and returned to Rome, where he was quickly arrested and thrown into the  Mamertine Prison.

During his nine month stay in a frightful dungeon there, Peter is said to have converted his two jailers - Processus and Martinianus, who became Christian leaders - as well as forty-seven others.

**MARTYRDOM**

Peter's wife,[21] who had ministered to the women alongside Peter through the years, was also imprisoned.   Clement tells us that as she was led out ahead of Peter to be martyred, Peter called to her encouragingly and comfortingly, addressing her by name, Perpetua, and saying, "Remember, dear, our Lord."

Then Peter was led out across the Tiber to the quarter inhabited by the Jews and crucified most likely on the top of Mt Janiculum. Both Jerome and Eusebius tell us that he was crucified upside down at his own request, as he felt unworthy to die in the same manner as his Lord.

Paul was beheaded on the same day, and the traditional date for their deaths is the 29th June 67AD.

Paul would have been almost seventy and Peter about seventy-five years of age when these two great apostles of the Lord finally entered into their heavenly reward.

## MARK

After their deaths, Mark[22] is said to have made his way to Aquilea near the present city of Venice, taking a copy of his gospel with him.

Here he ministered for some months, leaving his gospel with the church there before he left.   This gospel was kept on show in the Cathedral of St Mark in Venice for many years.

Mark then made his way to Alexandria where, Atiya tells us, he was overjoyed to find the flock standing firm in their faith.   Their numbers had so multiplied that the Christians had built a considerable church in the suburban district of Baucalis, just outside Alexandria, where cattle grazed by the seashore.

Atiya continues, "The Coptic Church was one of the first on record to have a truly established church with a complete hierarchial framework. Even in the time of Mark, the first patriarch of Alexandria, the church seems to have had a bishop, presbyters and deacons. One of the three main liturgies used in the coptic church was that composed by Mark and perfected by Cyril the Great".

Mark was not allowed to enjoy the fruits of his labours for very long though. In 68AD Easter fell on the 25th April, the same day as the Serapis festival. Spreading rumours that the Christians threatened to overthrow the pagan deities, the furious mob which had gathered in the Serapion descended on the Christians while they were celebrating Easter at Baucalis.

Mark was seized, dragged through the streets by a rope around his neck, and then incarcerated for the night. In the morning they repeated the performance until Mark gave up the ghost. A sudden downpour caused the people to disperse hurriedly, and the Christians were able to retrieve Mark's body.   They interred it in a grave they had carved in the rock under the altar of the church.

Mark was only about fifty-five when he died. Yet his gospel has gone on speaking to multitudes down through the centuries.

Shortest of the four gospels but full of action, Mark is often the first New Testament book to be translated into a new language. Embodying the teaching of his spiritual father, Peter, Mark's gospel has been the means of bringing people of many lands to a simple faith in the Saviour.

For both Peter and Mark, the words, 'he being dead yet speaks' remain as wonderfully true today as they did in the first century.

## REFERENCES FOR PETER

1. John 1:40-42, 21:15-16, Matthew 8:14, Eusebius (W) p 140, Schaff p 315, Morgan p 129 (Alford), James p 471, Halley p 465, I Corinthians 9:5, Fausset pp 560, 562, (Johanna, Perpetua), Schaff pp 314-315

2. John 21:15-17, Acts 1:15, 2:14, 43, 5:15,

3. Eusebius (W) pp 72 (James), Acts 8:15-25, 9:32-42,10:1-48, Galatians 1:18, Atiya p 394, Acts 11:19, Matthew 15:21-28, Mark 3:8, Luke 6:17-19, McBirnie pp 46-54, Latourette p 70, Thiede pp 167-169, Atiya p 394, Taylor p 60, Acts 11:19-26, McBirnie p 144

4. Acts 12:17, 13:1-3, Henry & Scott p 552, McBirnie p 62 , Wenham p 156, Thiede p 44

5. Eusebius (W) pp 85-88, 105, (Dionysius), Jerome p 361, Unger (Dict) p 695, Halley p 457, Fausset pp 452-453, Atiya p 26, Henry & Scott p 153, McBirnie pp 62, 67-68, Barclay p 15, Fausset p 562, Jackson p 244 (Hippolytus), Thiede (L) pp 43-49

6. Mark 14:51-52, Atiya p 26, Acts 10:45, 12:12-17, 19-23,McBirnie pp 252-253, Jerome pp 361, 364, 370, Eusebius (W) pp 81-83, Josephus Antiquities Bk XIX : 8, Acts 12:1,19-23, Fausset pp 285-286, I Peter 5:13, Unger (Dict) p 695, Fausset p 451, Halley p 457

7. Jowett pp 113, 115, 118, 158, 173, 174, 175, Lewis pp 25-26, II Tim 4:21, Thiede (L) p 190, Morton (P) p 408, Fausset p 133, Morgan pp 103-105

8. McBirnie pp 58, 59 (Whithorn), 61, Jowett pp 72, 76, 99-102, 117, 144,174- 175, Morgan pp 93-97, 161, Suetonius p 196,

Dio Cassius Bk 60 p 14,   Tacitus Annals 13:30,  p 268-299 (Pomponia), Jackson pp 248- 249,  Morton (P) p 408

9.  Jowett pp 175, 207, (Cornhill),  McBirnie p 59,  Taylor p 243

10. Works of Philo p XI, (death), Eusebius (W) pp 89-91, Jerome pp 364, 365

11. Eusebius (W) pp 152, 210, 254, 265,  Jerome pp 361, 364,  Halley p 458, McBirnie pp 70, 251 (Dead Sea Scrolls), 253-254, Fausset pp 452-453, Wenham pp 140-141, 146-148, 158-159, 171,  Matt Henry p 162, Bruce (NT Hist) p 375, ft/nt 1, Thiede (L) pp 41-49, Thiede (P) Pp 98,102

12. Atiya pp 225-28, McBirnie pp 252-257, Jackson pp 42, 271, Eusebius(W) pp 89-91, 103, 124 (Annianus),  Jerome p 364, Wenham pp 174-175,  Matt Henry p 162,  Unger (Dict) p 695

13. Eusebius(W)p95, (S)p1-2,  Suetoniusp(P) 202, Int Std Bible Enc p 217 Fausset p 45 (Claudius), Halley p637

14. Acts 15:22, 30-41, Galatians 2:11-14,  Jerome p 361,   Stoker p 115, Atiya pp 171-172,  McBirnie pp 53-56,  I Corinthians 1:12, Enc Brit Vol VII p 910 (First Bishop),  Unger (Dict) p 1025

15. McBirnie pp 253, 259-262,  Acts 15:36-39, 13:4-12,  Fausset pp 77-78, Jowett p 172,  Morton(P) pp119-121, 126-130 Eusebius (W) p 128 (Euodius & Ignatius)

16. McBirnie pp 63, 144-145, 254,  Edersheim p 14, Thompson's NIV p 1565, Unger (Dict) p 850, 1025,  Fausset p 451, 562 (Epistle), I Peter 5:1,13

17. Colossians 4:10,  Morton (P) pp 405-407,   Stoker p 109

18. Forbes p 88, 92-93, Tacitus Annals Bk XII: 29-37 (speech),  pp 264-268,  Jowett p 106, 114, 185,  Morgan pp 91-106, Fausset p 435, 691, 133 - Martial iv:13, xi:54,  Morton p 408, Eusebis (W) 107, II Timothy 4:21 Lewis p 26

19. Romans 16:10, Jowett pp 186-189, Stoker p 1

20. Morgan p 179 (ft/note), Lewis p 122-4, Eusebius (W) p 105, Jackson pp 210, 246, II Peter 3:1, 1:13-15,  McBirnie p 64-65, Thiede (L) pp 190-191,  Morton p 408, Tacitus : Annals XV 44:2-8, Eusebius (S) p 2-3 , Wenham p 154, Jackson p 246 (Irenaeus), Eusebius (S), p 146 (Mur Frag), 4 (Clement), Morgan p 156,158-161, Thiede (L) p143,  Peter to Britain : Lewis p 26, II Peter 3:1, 1:13,15

21. Eusebius (W) pp 104, 105, 107 +ft/nt, 140 (wife),  Abbott p 223, McBirnie pp 63-66, 69-71,  Schaff p 292,  Unger (Dict) p 850, Fausset pp 560-562, Jowett pp 176-177,   Barclay pp 22-24,  Fox (Z) p 4, (B) p 9, Thiede (L) p 201 (aged 75), Eusebius (S) p 6,  (W) p 105,  Morton (P) p 401

22. McBirnie pp 256-257,  Nicephorus HE. 11:43,  Fausset p 451, Fox (Z) p 3, Unger(Dict) p 695,  Atiya p 122

# JOHN

John is generally considered to have been the youngest of the twelve apostles and was probably about twenty-eight years old when he first followed Jesus. His father, Zebedee, was sufficiently wealthy to employ hired servants. His mother, Salome, was one of the women who ministered to Jesus and the apostles from their personal means. John himself had a house in Jerusalem. So the family was apparently reasonably well off.[1]

Andrew[2] and John were disciples of John the Baptist and were the first of the twelve to spend time alone with Jesus. Probably both became convinced that Jesus was the Messiah after that memorable day they spent with him. No doubt John also brought his own brother, James, to Jesus, although he only tells us what Andrew did.

Within a few days, John and the other five early disciples of Jesus witnessed his first miracle of turning water into wine at the marriage in Cana, and John tells us, "his disciples believed in Him."

Soon after this they accompanied Jesus back to Jerusalem for the Passover of 27AD. During this first Passover of his ministry, Jesus performed amazing miracles in the temple courts and because of them many people believed in Him.

## NICODEMUS

One of these was a leading Pharisee and member of the Sanhedrin named Nicodemus[3] who came secretly at night to talk with Jesus. Jesus was apparently staying with John at his town house and John most likely escorted Nicodemus up the outside stairs to the simply furnished Aliyah or guest chamber on the roof.  It seems John then remained at a discreet distance while Jesus and Nicodemus had their momentous discussion. Nicodemus was no doubt looking for a political Messiah who would overthrow the Romans and set up

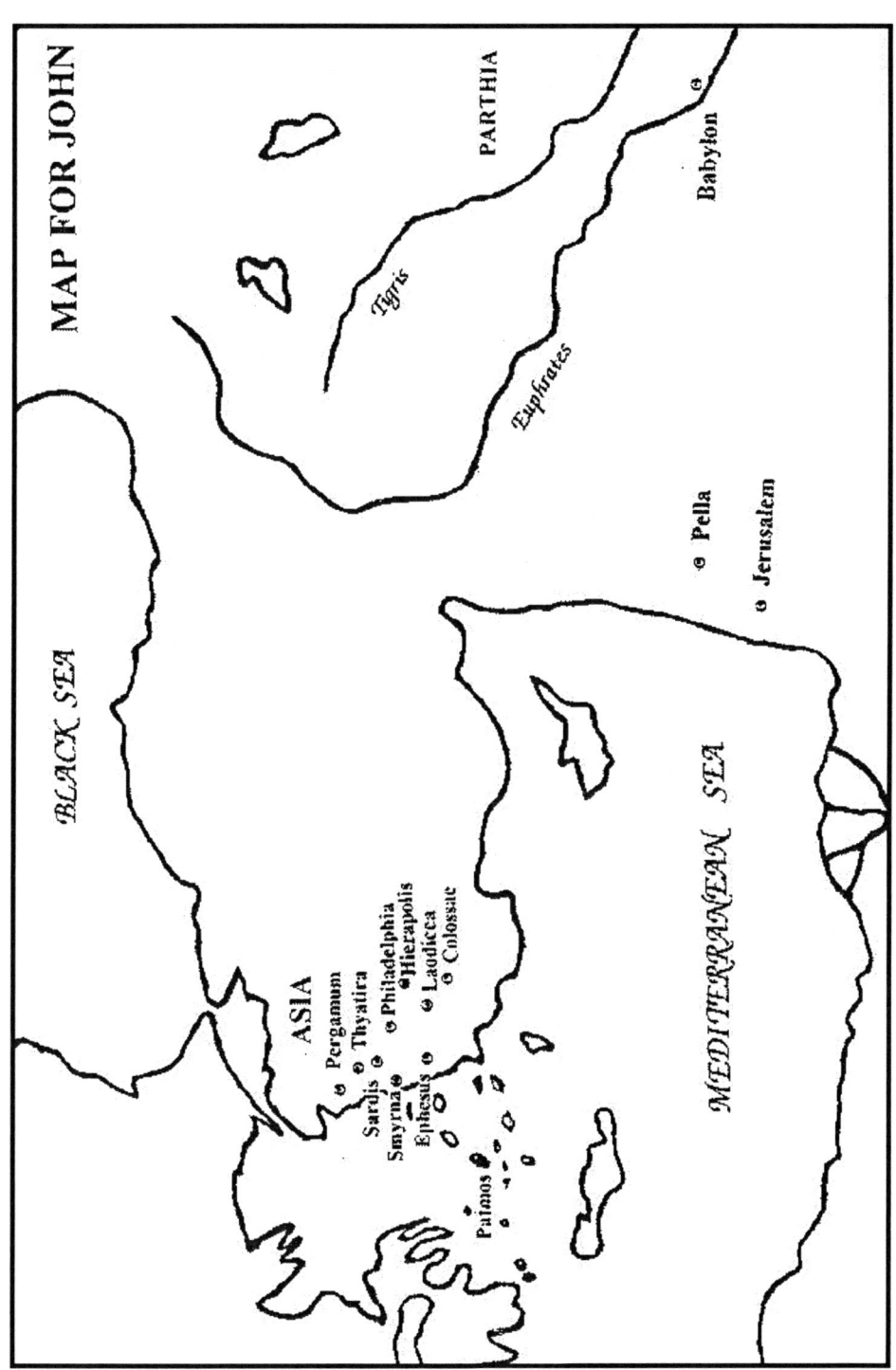

MAP FOR JOHN

BLACK SEA

PARTHIA

Tigris

Euphrates

Babylon

Pella

Jerusalem

ASIA

Pergamum

Thyatira

Sardis

Philadelphia

Smyrna

Hierapolis

Ephesus

Laodicea

Colossae

Patmos

MEDITERRANEAN SEA

Godly Jewish rule in Jerusalem. But Jesus cut across this idea by telling Nicodemus that His kingdom was not of this world but was to be a personal and spiritual one established in the heart of each individual who believed in Him and was 'born again' of His spirit.

Edersheim considers the account of what passed between the two men reads like the report of one who was present at the time and who may even have taken notes as he listened.

If this is so then John probably also heard the spring wind referred to by Jesus, blowing and whistling along the street below.

Two years after this interview, we find Nicodemus speaking up in Jesus' defence at a meeting of the Sanhedrin.

## INNER THREE

The first time we meet John he is in the company of Andrew. Before long, however, we find him with his older brother James and Peter as part of an inner group of three[4] who received special training from Jesus. They alone of the twelve were present at the raising of Jairus' daughter and later at the transfiguration of Jesus. In the Garden of Gethsemane Jesus chose these three to specially watch and pray with Him during his time of anguished prayer.

## LOVE AND THUNDER

Early in his ministry Jesus called James and John Sons of Thunder,[5] and on several occasions they backed this up. One time they wanted to call fire down on a Samaritan village which had refused to provide food and lodging for Jesus. They also wanted to stop a man who was casting out devils in Jesus' name, and later they requested that they might sit on the right and left hand of Jesus.

However, tempered with this hot headedness and bold ambition, was a deep-seated love for Jesus and a dedication to his cause.

John often designates himself as 'the disciple whom Jesus loved'.[6] At the Last Supper he reclined on Jesus' breast. Then in the garden, when all the other disciples forsook Jesus and fled, John showed his devotion by following the soldiers to the house of Caiaphas. Being known to the servants of the High Priest, possibly through supplying the household with fish, John was allowed into the Council chamber while Peter remained outside on the porch.

# MARY

John was also the only disciple with the courage to stand by Jesus during His long, agonising hours on the cross. It was from the cross that Jesus committed his mother into John's care. John took Mary[7] back to his own house in Jerusalem and Nicephorus tells us that he cared for her there like a son until the day of her death.

Irenaeus, Matthew Henry and others consider this to have been fifteen years after the resurrection, or about 45AD, when Mary would have been around sixty-five years of age.

Another account claims that Mary accompanied John to Ephesus and later died there. This would make her somewhere around ninety years of age when she died. Although this is possible, it would be unlikely for a person who had lived through all Mary had to survive to this late age. Both places purport to show her tomb, but the one in Jerusalem seems the more likely of the two.

## JOHN AND PETER

Shortly before the crucifixion Jesus assigned Peter and John to secretly prepare the Passover meal for the twelve at the home of John Mark and his mother Mary. From then on we find Peter and John paired together in various situations.

On the morning of the resurrection, Peter was apparently staying at John's house when the women came with their astounding news. Thirty-one year old John easily outran the no doubt heavier, thirty-eight year old Peter[8] to the tomb. John tells us that when he saw the grave clothes 'he believed', while most of the other disciples still doubted.

When Jesus prepared breakfast on the beach for seven of his disciples, it was John who first recognised the Lord from the boat but it was Peter who dived into the sea and swam to Jesus.

In the book of Acts John is generally seen in company with Peter. However, in the healing of the man at the Gate Beautiful, when arrested by the temple police and in visiting Samaria Peter always seemed to act as spokesman for the pair. Yet when Paul visited Jerusalem some years later, probably for the council of 49AD, he refers to John as one of the pillars or leaders of the Jerusalem church, along with Peter and James the brother of Jesus.

Apart from his trip to Samaria with Peter, John doesn't seem to have left Jerusalem for any protracted trips at least until after the death of Mary, probably around 45AD.

When Paul is arrested in Jerusalem in mid-58AD, however, John is not mentioned, and it is thought he could have been visiting the churches in Parthia at this time, as mentioned by Augustine.

## PELLA

After the martyrdom of James, the brother of Jesus in 62AD, John appears to have taken over the leadership of the Jerusalem church.

Then in mid-66AD, just before the besieging of Jerusalem by Roman troops, Eusebius tells us, the Christians were warned by the Lord in a prophetic message to flee to the town of Pella[9]. One of the ten cities of the Decapolis, many people there had believed on Jesus during his extensive  ministry throughout that area. At Pella the Christians were able to escape the terrible destruction that awaited Jerusalem and its inhabitants.

Yet John and his companions would have had the heart-breaking experience of hearing of synagogues destroyed by the advancing Romans, and of seeing life as they had always known it, both in Galilee and Judea, fast disappearing.

Following the fall of Jerusalem in 70 AD, the Jews generally were banned by the Roman army from returning to the ruined city.

However, a small group of Christians, under the leadership of Symeon,[10] son of Clopas, younger brother of James the Less, and cousin of Jesus, were allowed to return.  They restored the home of John Mark which became their meeting place and headquarters.

## EPHESUS

With the death of Peter and Paul on the 29th June 67AD, John became one of the few remaining apostles. He was encouraged by his fellow-Christians to move to Ephesus,[11] mid-way between Jerusalem and Rome, and by then one of the leading centres of Christianity.

Chief city of the Roman Province of Asia, Ephesus vied with Antioch and Alexandria as one of the top three cities of the eastern Mediterranean world. Located near the mouth of the Cayster River, Ephesus boasted a population of more than a quarter of a million people.

It was also home to one of the seven wonders of the ancient world, the Artemision.  This imposing marble temple of the Greek goddess

Artemis, or Diana as the Romans called her, was one of the largest buildings of antiquity.

Here, with the assistance of Timothy, pastor or Bishop of the Church of Ephesus, John had the oversight of churches for more than one hundred and sixty kilometers around, reaching as far as Pergamum to the north and Colossae in the east.

## GOSPEL

It was probably around 68AD that, Jerome[12] and others tell us, the leaders of the churches of Asia, no doubt including Timothy, asked John to commit to writing the things he had told them about Jesus which were not included in the other three gospels.   They particularly wanted  the special teaching which Jesus had given to his disciples on the night of the Last Supper. According to the Muratorian Fragment,  John asked them to fast and pray with him for three days to seek the Lord's will in the matter. God confirmed this to them through the apostle Andrew, and John set about writing his gospel.

Some time after this John also wrote his three epistles to help and encourage Christians in the area.

## DECADE OF MARTYRS

The decade between 60 and 70 AD[13,] however, must have been a very sad one for John.   Beginning with the stoning of Barnabas on the 11th June 58AD, this was followed by the death of  Lazarus in 60AD,  the martyrdom of  Thomas on the 21st December 60AD in India, and the crucifixion of Simon the Zealot in Britain on the 10th May 61AD.

Then at Passover in April of 62AD, James the brother of Jesus, whom John would have worked with for many years, was cast from the pinnacle of the temple by the Sanhedrin and had his life ended by a fuller's club.

In 64AD Matthias was killed by an angry mob in Judea, and on the 28th October 66AD Jude Thaddaeus was martyred in Armenia.

Peter and Paul were martyred in Rome on the 29th June 67AD, and Philip was crucified soon after on the 15th November 67AD. Mark was brutally murdered in Alexandria on the 25th April 68AD, followed by Bartholomew on the 24th August and Matthew on the

21st September 68AD.

Andrew was apparently the last of the twelve to suffer martyrdom in Patras on the 30th November 69AD.

Also around this time, Fox tells us, Erastus of Corinth, Aristarchus the Macedonian, Trophimus of Ephesus, as well as Joseph Barsabas and Ananias, bishop of Damascus, both of the seventy, were all martyred for their testimony to Jesus.

Added to this was the heartbreaking destruction of the Temple in Jerusalem and all that had constituted life as John had known it for over seventy years.

## ASIAN MINISTRY

There are many inspiring stories however, of John's ministry during the thirty years he spent in Asia.[14] One of the highlights must have been the conversion and training of the young men Papias and Polycarp. In later years these two became bishops of Hierapolis and Smyrna respectively and were widely respected as leaders of the church after John's death.

Clement of Alexandria relates a story which shows both John's caring heart and also his "Son of Thunder" strength of character.

While visiting a certain congregation John saw a young man of refined appearance and ardent spirit. John made a point of entrusting his care to the local bishop until he should again visit that church.

The bishop did his best, but the young man fell into bad company and eventually joined a violent robber band. When John returned and asked to see the youth he was distressed to hear the bad news. Calling for a horse and guide, John rode to the robbers' headquarters and was captured by the sentries.

When the young man recognised John, he was smitten with shame and fled from his presence. Despite his old age, John pursued him, offering to give his own life if the young man would only turn back to God.

Hearing this, the young man threw away his weapons and fell to his knees, trembling and in tears. With bitter contrition he repented. John prayed with him and led him back to the Saviour. Then John took him back to the church where he personally kept a keen eye on the lad.

The young man became so changed by Christ that in time he

became the bishop of that same congregation.

## PARTRIDGE

Another story related by John Cassian shows the great wisdom and peace that John had attained in old age.

One day John was gently stroking a partridge with his hands when a philosopher approached him in the dress of a hunter. The philosopher was astonished that a man of such great fame and reputation should demean himself with so trivial a pastime.

John said to him, "What is that you are carrying in your hand?"

"A bow," the man replied.

John asked why the hunter didn't keep the bow continually bent and taut. The hunter explained that if he did so, the strain placed upon the bow would limit its usefulness when he needed it to shoot arrows at a target.

"So, my lad," said John, "do not let this slight and short relaxation of my mind disturb you. Unless its rigour is sometimes relieved by some recreation, the spirit would lose its spring owing to the unbroken strain, and would be unable, when need required, to implicitly follow what was right."

## CERINTHUS

A more humorous incident related by Irenaeus shows the 'Thunder' side of John's character. There was in Ephesus an arch-heretic called Cerinthus who taught that Jesus never had a flesh and blood body but was only a phantom. One day when John went to the public bath house to bathe, he heard that Cerinthus was there.

"Let us flee," he exclaimed, "lest the bath-house fall down, because Cerinthus, the enemy of truth is therein.!"

## PATMOS

In early 95AD John was arrested by the Emperor Domitian[15] and taken to Rome.

Here, Jerome tells us, John was forced to drink hemlock, but when it had no ill effect on him, a criminal standing nearby was given some and died immediately.

Domitian decided that if he couldn't kill John in this way he would banish him to the penal colony on the island of Patmos, in the Aegean Sea, ninety-six kilometers south-west of Ephesus. About sixteen kilometers long by nine kilometers wide, the rocky, treeless island of Patmos was home to hundreds of slaves of Rome who worked in the mines without respite until they died in their chains.

Although John was now in his mid-nineties, it seems he was soon winning so many of his fellow slaves to the Lord that the authorities removed him to solitary confinement in a rugged cave on the wind-swept southern slope of the island.

A fissure in the roof allowed a shaft of light into the cave. One Lord's Day, or Sunday, John tells us, he was praying in the spirit. Apparently he was kneeling on the cave's rocky floor beside a large stone which he used to lean on to push himself up. Suddenly Jesus appeared to him in all his glory and told John to write what he saw.

The Lord then proceeded to unfold to John in amazing visions the contents of the book of Revelation.

Especially poignant to John must have been the special messages to the seven Asiatic churches which had been under his care for many years. It has been suggested that the 'Angel' of the church at Ephesus may have been Timothy.

If so, he, and probably the church itself, seems to have soon regained their 'first love' for the Lord.

Within ten years of the death of John, Pliny reported to the Emperor Trajan that the Christians of Ephesus had become so numerous that the heathen temples were almost deserted.

## DOMITIAN AND NERVA

Irenaeus states that the Apocalypse or Revelation was given to John towards the end of Domitian's reign. Not long after John had completed the Revelation, Domitian's wife discovered her name was on the emperor's death list. She immediately conspired with others on the list to have Domitian[16] himself assassinated.

Suetonius tells us that Stephanus, Flavia Domitilla's administrator, had feigned an arm injury and gone around for several days with it swathed in woollen bandages. Then, on the appointed day, Stephanus sent word to Domition that he had uncovered a plot against the emperor. As Domitian perused the document he had handed him, Stephanus drew a concealed dagger from within his arm bandages and plunged it into the tyrant.

Domitian was slain on the 18th September 96AD at the age of

forty-four after a reign of fifteen years. On that same day the senate elected as emperor a virtuous, God-fearing sixty-five year old man by the name of Nerva. Nerva quickly revoked all honours Domitian had bestowed on unworthy men, and all unjust sentences on innocent people.

Among them, Clement of Alexandria tells us, was the apostle John, released from almost eighteen months' confinement on the island of Patmos. John returned to Ephesus, where, in spite of his advanced age, he continued to oversee and encourage the fast growing churches of Asia for the next two years.

## TIMOTHY

For nearly thirty years now Timothy[17] had been John's valued co-worker and friend. A convert of the apostle Paul while probably still in his late teens, Timothy had later ministered to and assisted Paul during his almost three years of ministry in Ephesus from 54 to 57AD. During this time Timothy had seen God work special miracles through Paul with many people throughout the whole area won to the Lord.

About two years after Paul's release from his first period of imprisonment, he placed Timothy in charge of the church at Ephesus as his deputy, with instructions to appoint elders and deacons and to deal with any heresies in the church.

Not long after this Paul was again arrested and imprisoned, and on his death in June 67AD, it seems Timothy, according to Eusebius, became the first Bishop of the church at Ephesus while still in his mid thirties.

Some months later John arrived to assist the young pastor, yet Timothy appears to have continued in his role as bishop or pastor of Ephesus for the next thirty years.

Then in the spring of 97AD, Nicephorus tells us, as Timothy was returning home from a visit across town, he was caught up in a great pagan procession in honour of the goddess Diana. Timothy boldly reproved the revellers for their idolatry and immorality, at which the maddened crowd fell on him and mercilessly pounded him with their clubs.

For two days the faithful pastor lingered on in pain before finally dying of his injuries at around sixty-five years of age.

## DEATH OF JOHN

Timothy's death would have been a cruel loss to John. His strength began to fail quickly now. Before long his disciples had to carry him to church in their arms. Too weak to say much, Jerome tells us, still at each service John would exhort his followers with the words, "Little children, love one another." Eventually his disciples tired of hearing this and asked John why he kept saying the same words. "It is the Lord's command," he replied, "and if this alone be done, it is enough."

Finally, on the 26th September, 98AD,[18] the apostle John, Son of Thunder and disciple whom Jesus loved, passed peacefully into the presence of the Lord he had served so faithfully for more than sixty-eight years.

At almost one hundred years of age, John had outlived by nearly thirty years virtually all those who had walked with the Lord in the flesh, and many later disciples as well.

John's tomb can still be seen at Ephesus to this day.

## REFERENCES FOR JOHN

1.  Fausset p 384, Schaff pp 563, 569, Mark 1:19-20, 15:40-41, Luke 8:3, John 19:26-27, Morton (M) p 219, Barclay p 31, Halley pp 465-466
2.  John 1:35-42, 2:1-11, 13, 23
3.  John 3:1-21, 7:50-52, Edersheim (M) p382, McBirnie p 108, Halley p 528
4.  Matthew 17:1-3, 26:36-38, Mark 5:22,37, 9:2, Luke 22:7-13
5.  Mark 3:17, 9:38, Luke 9:51-56, Schaff pp 570-571
6.  John 13:23,-24, 19:26, 20:2, 21:7,20, John 18:1-28, McBirnie p 109
7.  John 19:26-27, Barclay p 32 (Nicephorus EH 2:2), Schaff p 585, Henry & Scott p 552, McBirnie p 110 (Niceph EH 2:2), James p197
8.  John 20:2-9, 21:7-21, Acts 3:1,11, 4:13, 8:14, 15:1-23, Schaff p 585, Galatians 1:18-19, 2:9, Acts 21:17-19, McBirnie p 115 (Parthia)
9.  Eusebius (W) p 111,128, (S) pp 6-7 (Epiphanius) Morton (M) p 33, John 10:42, Unger (A:NT) pp 116, 139
10. Eusebius (W) pp 123-124, 128, 142-143, 145, 181

11. Eusebius(W) p 107,    Fausset p 384, Halley pp 700-701, Unger (A:NT) pp 249-263, Acts 19:1-41

12. Eusebius (W) pp 132-133,   Eusebius (S) p 145, Fausset p 385, Halley p 528, McBirnie pp 116-117 (Jerome),  Jerome p 364-365

13. Fox (Z) p 2-6

14. Eusebius (W) pp 128-131, 138-139,149 Barclay pp 33-35, (Jerome) McBirnie pp 113-116, Fausset pp 384-385

15. Jerome p 364-365,    Barclay p33,  Fox (Z) p 5,  Schaff p 592, Eusebius (W) pp 125-127, (S) p 9 (Patmos & Irenaeus), Revelation 1:9, McBirnie pp 110-112, 116-117,  Halley p 701,  Unger (Dict) p 830, Fausset pp 543, 604-606 (Irenaeus & Victorinus)

16. Eusebius (W) p 124-128, (S) p 9,  Abbott p 19,  Suetonius pp 310-312, McBirnie p 112,   Thiede (L) pp 188-189

17. Eusebius (W) p 109,  Fausset pp 689- 690 (Nicephorus EH 3:11), Fox (Z) p 7,  I Timothy 1:3, 3:1-13,   Halley p 632

18. Eusebius (W) pp 128, 140-141, Fausset p 385, Barclay p 36 (Jerome - Love),  McBirnie pp 109, 117-119 (26th Sept), Fox (B) p 10 (100 years),  Henry p 304 (natural death)

# WHO WERE THE SEVENTY?

In Luke we read that not long before His crucifixion Jesus "appointed seventy[1] others also, and sent them two by two ahead of Him to every town and place where He was about to go." Some manuscripts give the number as seventy-two, but Eusebius and other early writers refer to them as "The Seventy".

Jesus gave them power to heal the sick and cast out devils. But when they returned elated over the results of their ministry, Jesus told them to rejoice more over the fact that their names were written in heaven.

Just who were these seventy disciples? Both Hippolytus and Dorotheus are said to have made out a list of the seventy, but Eusebius tells us that no complete list was available in his day. We only have indirect references to some of them in the writings of others. From these, we can ascertain the following information.

## BARNABAS

We are told by Eusebius and other writers that Barnabas[2] was the first or leader of the seventy. His given name was Joseph, but because of his caring nature and ability to teach, the apostles named him Barnabas, meaning Son of Encouragement.

Luke states that Barnabas was "a good man, full of the Holy Spirit and faith." He is said to have been of a commanding and dignified appearance, yet with a gracious manner. The Lycaonians thought that Barnabas was the imposing Greek god, Zeus, and Paul his spokesman, Hermes.

Apparently Barnabas had not been with Jesus continuously from the time of our Lord's baptism until His ascension, so he could not qualify as a replacement for Judas Iscariot.

Barnabas, his older brother Aristobulous and their Aunt Mary, mother of John Mark, all seem to have been quite wealthy. Barnabas sold land he owned on Cyprus and gave the proceeds to the church. Mary had an upper room large enough to hold one hundred and twenty people. She had at least two servants, Rhoda who answered the door to Peter on his release from prison, and a male servant who carried a water jar to show Peter and John where they were to prepare the Passover feast.

It is thought that Jesus probably made the arrangements for the Last Supper secretly through Barnabas so Judas could not inform the Sanhedrin before the appointed time.

Barnabas was a Levite from the island of Cyprus. In 12BC Herod the Great had leased the extensive copper mines in the mountains of Cyprus from Augustus and many Jews had moved there to either work in the mines or assist in their management.

It may be that the family of Barnabas had gained their wealth in connection with these mines. It would seem they had business interests in Rome as well, and it may have been these commitments that prevented Barnabas from spending his whole time with Jesus.

Early in his ministry, while on a visit to Rome, Barnabas is said to have converted Clement of Rome, who later became the third Bishop of Rome and a leading figure in the church after the death of most of the apostles.

It is thought that Barnabas may have attended the school of Gamaliel with Saul of Tarsus when they were younger men. He certainly took upon himself the responsibility of introducing the newly-converted Saul to the apostles as if he was familiar with the nature of the man and knew he could trust him.

Around 42AD the apostles sent Barnabas to check out the situation at Antioch, where Gentiles were being welcomed into the church. Seeing the need for deeper teaching, Barnabas went to Tarsus to get Paul and together they taught the new Christians for about a year. Then in 44AD they took gifts from the church at Antioch down to the poorer church members in Jerusalem. On their return they were accompanied by John Mark, the young cousin of Barnabas.

Shortly afterwards, Paul and Barnabas set out on their first missionary journey, with John Mark as their assistant or servant.

They are said to have walked from Salamis to Citium, where they encouraged the believers won to the Lord by Lazarus some ten years earlier. From there they proceeded to Paphos where they encountered the Jewish astrologer, Elymas Bar Jesus.

Mark apparently did not take too well to being told what to do by Paul and  soon  after this he returned home to Jerusalem.

From this time on both Paul and Barnabas are called apostles, and at the council of Jerusalem around 49AD, they were recognised as 'the apostles of the circumcision.'

When Paul and Barnabas had their disagreement over Mark in 50AD, Barnabas took Mark and sailed for his home town of Salamis on the island of Cyprus. From here the two laboured together for the Lord for about eight years, while also preaching the gospel in other places, including Milan.

Finally, Elymas Bar Jesus, whom Paul had caused to become temporarily blind, determined to wreak his vengeance on Barnabas. Rousing the Jews of Salamis against the apostle, they rushed him to the hippodrome where an angry mob stoned him to death.

That night Mark stole the body of his cousin and buried it secretly in a Roman tomb outside the city, with Barnabas' hands folded over a copy of Matthew's gospel on his breast.

Barnabas is said to have died on the 11th June 58AD at around 60 years of age.   A small chapel has been built over his tomb and can be seen in Salamis to this day.

## ARISTOBULUS

Older brother of Barnabas, his name means 'best counsellor'. Aristobulus[3] is said to have been one of the seventy, and to have received the Holy Spirit along with his brother and Joseph of Arimathea in the upper room on the Day of Pentecost. He is also said to have worked with Paul for a time and to have helped found the church in Rome, holding meetings in his own  home.

In his epistle to the Romans, however,  Paul sends greetings to those in  the 'household of Aristobulus', indicating that  the head of the household is    absent from them but not deceased.

The Martyrologies of the Greek Church for March 15th, says, "Aristobulus was one of the seventy disciples and a follower of St Paul the apostle, along with whom he preached the gospel ... and ministered to him. He was chosen by St Paul to be the missionary bishop to the land of Britain.... he converted many of them to Christianity. He was there martyred after he had built churches and ordained deacons and priests for the island."

Hippolytus, Bishop of the Greek church in Rome around 195AD, and Dorotheus, Bishop of Tyre, 303AD, both mention Aristobulus as "Bishop of Britain."

Haleca, Bishop of Augusta wrote, "The memory of many martyrs is celebrated by the Britons, especially that of St Aristobulus, one of the seventy disciples."

Adonis Martyrologia, for the 17th March, "Natal day of Aristobulus, Bishop of Britain, brother of St Barnabas the apostle... was sent to Britain, where, after preaching the truth of Christ and forming a church, .. he received martyrdom."

The British Genealogies of the Saints of Britain states, "These came with Bran the Blessed from Rome to Britain - Arwystli Hen, Ilid, Cyndaw, men of Israel, Maw or Manaw, son of Arwystli Hen." Morgan adds, "According to the genius of the British tongue, Aristobulus becomes Arwystli."

It also appears from this list that Manaw, the son of Aristobulus, accompanied him to Britain.

In the Silurian records Aristobulus is styled Confessor or Instructor to Bran the Blessed.

Jowett writes, "They (the group from Rome) arrived at Llan-ilid, Glamorganshire, erecting a church as a memorial. Aristobulus was installed as the first Bishop at Llan-ilid, with Bran remaining as chief High Priest of Siluria at Llandaff.

"In the Cymric language Aristobulus is known as Arwystli-Hen - or Aristobulus the aged. (He was probably near seventy years of age.)

"Aristobulus was well respected by the Silurians, but in his preaching zeal he journeyed far beyond the territory of the Silurian shield into the lands of the British Ordivices. To them he had come from Rome and their hatred for the Romans was bitter and black. They rose and slew him, on the 15th March 59AD.

"Aristobulus was the first British bishop and the only one martyred by the British people.

Near the source of the river Severn in Montgomeryshire there is a place called Arwystli, named after him, where Aristobulus is said to have suffered martyrdom. In 1908, during repairs to the church of St George in Glastonbury, a tombstone was discovered inscribed in Latin, "To Gaius Aristobulus, A Roman citizen."

## MATTHIAS

Sometime during their ten days of prayer between the ascension of Jesus and the Day of Pentecost, the apostles decided they should choose a replacement for Judas Iscariot. Quoting Psalm 109:8, "May another take his place of leadership," Peter encouraged them to choose from among them men who had been with Jesus from His baptism to his ascension.

Although Barnabas and Aristobulus are said to have been among the one hundred and twenty present, apparently neither had been with Jesus the whole time, no doubt due to business commitments.

The two names put forward were Matthias[4] and Joseph Barsabbas. The apostles prayed,  asking God to guide them to the one of His choice.   Then they cast lots and the choice fell on Matthias.  Jerome, Clement, Eusebius and Epiphanius all state that Matthias was one of the seventy.

Soon after the stoning of Stephen, Matthias is said to have gone with the other apostles to take the gospel to the Jews of the dispersion. He is said to have preached in Cappadocia, Colchis and Sebastopol, where he was apparently rescued by the apostle Andrew.   He also worked for a time in  Armenia, where he is credited with being one of five apostles to have founded the church in that country. He is then said to have preached in Damascus.

On his return to Judea, Matthias preached openly for a while. However, the Jewish leaders soon became antagonistic. They eventually had him stoned to death in the Judean city of Phaelon, possibly on the 24th February 64AD.

## JOSEPH BARSABBAS

The other person chosen as a possible replacement for Judas Iscariot was Joseph Barsabbas,[5] surnamed Justus because of his just way of life.

He is thought to have been the brother of Judas Barsabbas. In Acts Judas is described as a leading man among the brethren at

Jerusalem, a prophet, chosen with Silas to deliver the decision of the Jerusalem church council to the Gentile believers at Antioch. While there, Judas and Silas exhorted the brethren with many words and confirmed them in their faith.

Both Eusebius and Fox state that Joseph was one of the seventy. If the two were brothers then Judas may also have been in this group. Whatever their background, both men seem to have been very dedicated to the Lord.

Papias says he heard the daughters of Philip relating a story about Joseph Barsabbas. Apparently on one occasion Joseph was given a poisoned drink by his enemies, but under God's protection he suffered no ill effects.

In Fox's Book of Martyrs Joseph is said to have suffered martyrdom soon after Peter and Paul, around 68AD.

## ANANIAS OF DAMASCUS

When the Christians were persecuted following the death of Stephen, Ananias,[6] said by Fox and Syrian tradition to have been one of the seventy, returned to his native city of Damascus. He had not been there long when he received instructions from God in a vision to go to the house of Judas on Straight Street and pray for Saul. As Ananias knew all about Saul's activities in Jerusalem he was naturally reluctant to go.

However, after reassurance from God that Saul was a chosen instrument of His, Ananias obeyed.

He prayed for Saul's sight to be restored and for him to be filled with the Holy Spirit. Then he baptised him in water. No doubt the two men had long discussions in the ensuing days before Paul was forced to flee the city.

In recounting this story nearly thirty years later, Paul says Ananias was "a devout man according to the law, having a good report of all the Jews which dwelt there".

Unger and others tell us that tradition states that Ananias became Bishop of Damascus, serving the Lord faithfully for almost forty years.

Ananias was martyred not long after Peter and Paul, around 68AD by the Prefect of Damascus. His home continued to be used as a meeting place for Christians after his death. In later years a large church was built over it, but the original home of Ananias underneath is still used as a chapel to this day.

## STACHYS

In Paul's greetings to the Christians at Rome, he mentions "my dear friend Stachys".[7] Said by Hippolytus and Dorotheus to have been one of the seventy, Stachys seems to have travelled far in his service for the Lord.

After helping to establish the church at Rome, Stachys apparently joined Philip at Hierapolis where he served the Lord for about ten years, holding meetings in his own home.

The Acts of Philip tells us that Stachys was present in November 67AD when Philip and Bartholomew were arrested by the proconsul following the healing and conversion of his wife.

Stachys witnessed the two apostles being scourged and humiliated. Philip had his thighs and ankles pierced and was hung head down until he died as a martyr for his Lord. Bartholomew was hung by his hair, but was eventually released and moved on to Lycaonia.

The following year Andrew visited Hierapolis in the course of his travels. He ministered to the Christians there for a time, then with Stachys accompanying him, he moved on to Byzantium. Here the two worked together for some months establishing a strong church. Then before leaving, Nicephorus tells us, Andrew ordained Stachys as first bishop of Byzantium, where he served the Lord faithfully for many years.

## MARI

Mari[8] , said to have been one of the seventy, is claimed by the Church of the East as one of the founders of the church of Babylon, along with the apostles Peter, Thomas, Jude Thaddaeus and Simon the Zealot.

## ANDRONICUS AND JUNIAS

Two of Paul's kinsmen who were then living in Rome. Paul refers to them in his epistle to the Romans as "my relatives who have been in prison with me. They are outstanding among the apostles and they were in Christ before I was." As members of the seventy Andronicus and Junias[9] certainly would have been Christians before Paul.

Andronicus is said by Dorotheus to have preached in Spain and Hippolytos says he became Bishop of Pannonia.

## SOSTHENES

Paul says Sosthenes[10] was with him when he wrote to the Corinthians from Ephesus, and he designates him as 'our brother'. Eusebius says he was joint author with Paul of the first epistle to the Corinthians. He also states that Sosthenes was one of the seventy.

This would mean he was a different Sosthenes to the ruler of the synagogue in Corinth who brought Paul before Gallio.

## MAXIMIN

Around 36AD Maximin is said to have travelled in a boat with Joseph of Arimathea, Lazarus, Mary, Martha, Restitutus (the man born blind) and others to Marseilles. After spending a short time working there with the apostle Philip, Maximin is said to have moved on to Aix where he became the first bishop of that town.

Both Mary and Restitutus are said to have worked with him at Aix for some time before Restitutus moved on to become the first bishop of the Roman colony of Augusta Tricastinorum, where the church of St Restitut still stands.

Maximin is said to have been an older disciple, one of the seventy, and illustrious both by his power of miracles and of teaching. He gave himself to prayer and fasting that he might bring the people of that country to the knowledge and service of God.

The tombs of both Mary and Maximin are still shown at Aix to this day.

## REFERENCES FOR THE SEVENTY

1. **The Seventy** - Luke 10:1, 17, Eusebius (W) p 64
2. **Barnabas** - Eusebius (W) pp 64, 72, Acts 4:36, 9:27, 11:19-30, 14:8-12, Fox (Z) p 5, McBirnie pp 253, 259-261, Fausset pp 77-78, Morton (P) p 119-121, 126-130, NIV p 1565
3. **Aristobulous** - Unger (Dict) p 88, Romans 16:10, Fausset p 49, Stoker p 107, Morton (P) p 127, Zond Bible Dict p 70, Gladys Taylor p 65
4. **Matthias** - Acts 1:21-26, Eusebius (W) pp 64, 71, Fausset p 460, Unger (Dict) p 706, McBirnie pp 23-24, 207, 241-248

5. **Joseph Barsabbas** - Eusebius (W) p 151, Acts 1:21-26, 15:22-34, Fausset p 398, Fox (Z) p 6

6. **Ananias of Damascus** - Acts 9:1-19, 22:1-16, Fox (Z) p 6, Fausset p 36,  Morton (P) pp 39-40, Unger (Dict) p 49,  Eerdman's Bible Dict p 54

7. **Stachys** - Romans 16:9, Unger (Dict) p 1044, James p 448-450

8. **Andronicas and Junia** - Romans 16:7, Fausset p 37, Unger (Dict) p 52, NIV p 1565

9. **Mari** - McBirnie pp 144,  198,  Atiya p 295

10. **Sosthenes** - I Corinthians 1:1, Acts 18:17, Fausset p 661,   Eusebius (W) p 64

11. **Maximin** - J Taylor pp 89-90, 122, 197-198

# CHURCH FATHERS AND HISTORIANS

**JOSEPHUS,** Flavius (37-100). Father was governor of Galilee. Born and educated in Jerusalem, Josephus became a priest, then later a general in the Jewish army. Captured shortly before the fall of Jerusalem in 67AD, he encouraged the Jews to surrender rather than suffer wholesale massacre.

Taken to Rome by Vespasian and released, Josephus wrote "Wars of the Jews" and "Antiquities of the Jews". In them he mentions John the Baptist, Jesus and James the brother of Jesus as historical figures.

Of Jesus he writes : "Now there was about this time Jesus, a wise man, if it be lawful to call him a man, for he was a doer of wonderful works, a teacher ... he was the Christ, and when Pilate, at the suggestion of the principal men among us, had condemned him to the cross, ... He appeared alive again the third day ... and the tribe of the Christians, so named from him, are not extinct at this day." (ie 93-95AD).

**CLEMENT OF ROME**, (5(?) - 101AD).     Converted by the preaching of Barnabas in Rome soon after the resurrection.     Was a companion of both Peter and Paul and was well acquainted with John.    He is mentioned by Paul in Philippians 4:3.

 Bishop of Rome from 91-100AD, Clement wrote his epistle to the Corinthians while John was on Patmos in 95AD.

This epistle was so well received that it was read in the churches down to the fourth century and was included at the back of the Alexandrian manuscript of the Bible.   Clement writes of Paul's visit to 'the extremities of the west' (Spain and possibly Britain), and the martyrdom of Peter and Paul.

He was condemned to the mines and suffered martyrdom in the third year of Trajan, 101AD.

**IGNATIUS** (67-110AD)   Pupil of John, Bishop of Antioch (after Peter and Euodius). On a visit to Antioch, the emperor Trajan ordered Ignatius to be thrown to the wild beasts at Rome.

On the way there Ignatius wrote seven letters - six to various churches and one to Polycarp. One was to the church at Rome, begging them not to try and procure his pardon as he longed for the honour of dying for his Lord.

We still have copies of these letters and they are most inspiring.

**POLYCARP** (69-155AD)   Pupil of John, Bishop of Smyrna for many years.   Became a 'father-figure' to the church after the death of the apostle John in 98AD.   In the persecution ordered by the emperor, Polycarp was arrested and brought before the governor.

When offered his freedom if he would curse Christ, he replied, "Eighty and six years have I served Christ and he has done me nothing but good; how then could I curse Him, my Lord and Saviour?"

He was burned at the stake at Smyrna. His inspiring epistle to the Phillipians, written around 110AD,  is still extant.

**PAPIAS**   (70 (?) - 155AD)   Another pupil of John, became Bishop of Hierapolis, about a hundred and sixty kilometers east of Ephesus.   Philip had ministered  and was martyred here,  probably before Papias was born, but Papias states that he heard the daughters of Philip relating miracles in the lives of  Joseph Barsabas and the wife of Manaen.

Papias wrote a book titled, "Explanation of the Lord's Discourses" which was extant down to the 13th century, but now only fragments remain in quotations in Irenaeus, Eusebius and others.   In it he says he made it a point to inquire of the elders the exact words of Jesus. He suffered martyrdom at Pergamum around the same time as Polycarp.

**TACITUS** (55-120AD)   Roman Historian.   Tacitus wrote a number of detailed histories including "The Annals of Imperial Rome", "The Histories" and "The Agricola and the Germania". From these we gain much of our knowledge of events in the Roman

Empire of the first century AD.

Regarding the great fire of Rome which took place under Nero in 64AD, Tacitus writes : "Nero fastened the guilt, and inflicted the most exquisite tortures on the group popularly known as Christians. Christ, from whom the name had its origin, suffered the extreme penalty during the reign of Tiberius at the hands of one of our procurators, Pontius Pilate, and a most mischievous superstition, thus checked for the moment, again broke out, not only in Judea, but even in Rome."

**SUETONIUS** (69-140AD)  Early second century Latin historian. He practised briefly at the bar before becoming chief secretary to the Emperor Hadrian (117-138AD).  After being sacked for being impolite to the Empress Sabina, Suetonius devoted his time to writing numerous books on Roman life at the time.

His only extant book, however,  is the classical work, "The Twelve Caesars".  Along with the works of Tacitus, this book gives us a detailed account of the triumphs and foibles of  Roman rulers from Julius Caesar to Domitian.   In it Suetonius mentions Claudius expelling Jews from Rome in 49AD because of trouble caused by followers of one Chrestus (Christ).

**DIDACHE** or 'Teaching of the Twelve', written in Alexandria between 80 and 120AD, probably about 100AD.   It abounds in quotations from the New Testament books and shows a church still throbbing with missionary zeal.  "He that believeth and is baptised" was an important emphasis.  Although the early church denied its canonicity, it was nevertheless held in high regard.

**ARISTIDES**   a converted philosopher of Athens, wrote a "Defense of Christianity" to Hadrian  125AD  and to Antonius 137AD appealing for protection of Christians against persecution. He paid high tribute to "their true and noble creed and their pure and benevolent lives."

**JUSTYN MARTYR**   (100-167AD)    Born in Samaria of a Greek father, Justyn Martyr received a good education and travelled widely.  He studied philosophy, and in his youth saw a good deal of persecution of Christians.   Eventually he was converted to Christ and from then on he travelled in a philosopher's robe seeking to win men to the Savior.

Around 140AD he wrote a defense of Christianity addressed to the emperor.   In it he said, "already there is no race of men where prayers are not offered up in the name of Jesus."   One of the ablest men of his time, Justyn Martyr died for his faith at Rome in 167AD.

**TATIAN**  a Greek-Syrian Christian writer and missionary. About 160AD  he wrote a 'Harmony of the Four Gospels'.

**HEGESIPPUS**  (100-180AD) a Jewish-Christian Historian who wrote about 169AD.   In his fifth book about the lives and preaching of the apostles,  he gives a detailed account of the life and martyrdom of James the Lord's brother.   Eusebius says that he "quoted from Hegesippus on numerous occasions, using information gained from him to establish facts about the apostolic age".

**DIONYSIUS**, (100-180) Bishop of Corinth, in a letter to Soter, Bishop of Rome,   written 170AD, mentions that Peter and Paul founded the churches of both Rome and Corinth and that they were martyred at the same time.

**IRENAEUS** (130-200AD)    Brought up in Smyrna.   Pupil of Polycarp and Papias.   Travelled widely.   Became Bishop of Lyons, Gaul in 177AD.   Noted chiefly for his five books against Gnostics. He quotes from  most of the New Testament books as scripture, which in his time had come to be known as 'The Gospels and the Apostles'.   He died a martyr in 200AD.

**BARDAISAN** (154-222) , of Edessa, is the 'father' of Christian Syriac literature.   According to Epiphanius he was a confessor.

**CASIUS Dio,** (160-post 229), Roman consul in 211 and 229. Wrote in Greek a History of Rome from the beginning to AD 229 in 80 books.

**HIPPOLYTUS**, born about 160AD, the most learned member of the Roman Church of that period, was probably Bishop of the Greek church in Rome. He had heard Irenaeus preach. He was the author of many works which Eusebius says were of the 'highest literary merit'. In "The Answer to all the Heresies" he quotes from the writings of the apostles and gives many details of their lives and ministries.

**TERTULLIAN** (160-230AD) of Carthage, a pagan Roman lawyer. After his conversion he became a distinguished defender of Christianity. He speaks of the Christian scriptures as the "New Testament" (a title which first appeared in the writing of an unknown author about 193AD). In Tertullian's extant writings there are 1800 quotations from New Testament books.

**THE MURATORIAN FRAGMENT,** written in Rome about 170AD, contains a list of the Christian scriptures, and details on how the different books of the New Testament were written.

**PANTAENUS** leading Christian teacher in charge of the school to train Christian workers at Alexandria 185AD. He was sent as a missionary to India where he was shown a copy of Matthew's Gospel in Hebrew, said to have been taken there by Bartholomew. This he took back to Alexandria with him.

**CLEMENT OF ALEXANDRIA** (150-211AD) Followed Pantaenus as head of the Christian school and had to flee because of persecution in 202AD. Wrote at least five main works in which are found details of the lives and ministries of the apostles.

**ORIGEN** (185-254AD) The most learned man of the ancient church. A great traveller and a voluminous writer, employing at times as many as twenty copyists.

Two-thirds of the New Testament is quoted in his writings. He lived in Alexandria where his father, Leonidas, suffered martyrdom.

Origen followed Clement as head of the school in 202AD, and many heretics and philosophers attended, many of them becoming converted to Christ. Many of his pupils became martyrs for their faith. In his later years he went to Palestine where he suffered martyrdom at the age of 69 as a result of imprisonment and torture under Decius.

**CYPRIAN,** (200-258) of Carthage, converted in 246 and chosen as Bishop of Carthage 249. His letters are a most important historical source. He died a martyr on 14th September 258AD.

**DOROTHEUS,** Bishop of Tyre around 303AD wrote his 'Synopsis de Apostol' in which he gives details of the lives of the apostles. He is also said to have prepared a list of the seventy disciples sent out by Jesus.

**EUSEBIUS** (264-340AD)   Father of church history.   Bishop of Caesarea at the time of Constantine's conversion.   Had great influence with Constantine.  Wrote an "Ecclesiastical History - from Christ to the Council of Nicaea," and a "Life of Constantine."  He traced the movements of the twelve apostles and other early Christian leaders as best he could, quoting all known traditions and stories of their activities.

**JEROME** (340-420AD)   Most learned of the Latin fathers. Educated at Rome, of a Christian family, travelled widely.   Lived for a time in the desert near Antioch, then went to Constantinople and then Rome.

In 385AD he settled in Bethlehem in the former house of Ruth and Boaz, above the cave where it is believed Jesus was born.

He lived there for thirty years and translated the whole Bible into the Latin version, known as the Vulgate.   This is the Bible of the Roman Catholic Church.   He also enlarged Eusebius' church history for the years 325-378AD.

**EPIPHANIUS,** (315-403)   In 367 was chosen as Bishop of Salamis, Cyprus, and Metropolitan of the whole island.   He knew Greek, Hebrew, Syriac, Coptic and Latin.     In his eighty books against heresies he mentions the apostles and others, including Lazarus.

**JOHN CHRYSOSTOM,** (345-407), "The golden-mouthed", a matchless orator, greatest preacher of his day, an expository preacher. Born at Antioch, became patriarch of Constantinople, preached to great multitudes in church of St Sophia.   A reformer, he displeased the king, was banished and died in exile.

**AUGUSTINE**  (354-430AD)   Bishop of Hippo, North Arica, from 395-430AD.   For thirty years he lived a sinful, godless life, then he was converted in answer to his mother's prayers.  He was a brilliant man, became a great theologian and writer, and served God faithfully until his death at 76.

**AMBROSE** (340-397AD)   Bishop of Milan.   Formerly a successful lawyer, then Governor of Milan, before becoming a presbyter and finally Bishop.
  He wrote commentaries on the scriptures and composed church music and hymns, some of which are in our hymnbooks to this day.

**SOCRATES,** (380-post 439), of Constantinople, a lawyer, wrote a history of the church from 305-439 in seven books in which he preserved many original documents.

**THEODORET,**   Bishop of Cyrus near Antioch in Syria, was born about 390AD.   Around 435AD he wrote his commentaries on St Paul where he states that Scythians, Indians and Britons, among others, accept the laws of Christ.

**SOZOMEN,**  fl c 440, from near Gaza in Palestine, wrote a history of the Church from 324-425 in nine books at Constantinople. He quotes some original documents not used by Socrates.

**NICEPHORUS,** (758-829AD) Patriarch of Constantinople and Byzantine historian, gives us many details of the apostles in his Ecclesiastical History.

# BIBILIOGRAPHY

ABBOTT John SC, History of Christianity, Published by George Stinson & Co, Portland, Maine, USA, 1883.

APOCRYPHA The, Published by Oxford University Press, Amen House, EC4, London.

APOCRYPHAL NEW TESTAMENT, The. Translated by Montague Rhodes James, published by Oxford at the Clarendon Press, Oxford, 1983.

APOSTOLIC FATHERS, The. Translated by J. B. Lightfoot & J. R. Harmer, Baker Book House, Grand Rapids, Michigan 49516, 1989.

ATIYA, Aziz S. A History of Eastern Christianity. Published by Methuen & Co Ltd, 11 New Fetter Lane, London, EC4, 1968.

BARCLAY, William. The Master's Men.SCM Press Ltd, London, 1959.

BRUCE, F. F., DD, FBA. New Testament History. Pickering & Inglis, 3 Beggarwood Lane, Basingstoke, Hants RG23 7LP, U:Kingdom, 1985.

BRUCE, F.F. The Spreading Flame. Wm B Eerdmans Publishing Co, 255 Jefferson Ave., SE, Grand Rapids, Michigan, 49503, USA, 1985.

BRUCE, F.F. The New Testament Documents. Inter-Varsity Press, 3 De Montfort Street, Leicester LE1 7GP, England, 1992.

CAREY, William. An Enquiry.

CHURCHILL, Winston S. A History Of The English-Speaking Peoples. Cassell & Co Ltd. London, 1956.

D'SOUZA, Rev Father Herman MA, M Ed. In The Steps of St. Thomas. Published by the Diocese of Mylapore, for the 19th Centenary celebrations of the arrival of St. Thomas in India, 31st July 1952.

EDERSHEIM, Alfred, DD, PhD. The Life and Times of Jesus the Messiah. Macdonald Publishing Co Ltd., Mclean, Virginia, 22102, 1883

EDERSHEIM, Alfred , DD, PhD.    Sketches of Jewish Social Life in the Times of Jesus. First published 1876.  Pub 1980 by Wm B Eerdmans, Grand Rapids, Michigan, USA.

ENCYCLOPAEDIA BRITANNICA, Macro and Micro, published by William Benton, 1974.

EUSEBIUS.    The History of the Church from Christ to Constantine, Translated by G. A. Williamson, Ausburg Publishing House, Minneapolis, Minnesota, 1975, reprinted from Penguin Classics, pub 1965.

EUSEBIUS, A New.    Edited by J Stevenson, Published by SPCK, Holy Trinity Church, Marylebone Road, London, NW1 4DU, 1957, 1983.

FALLOWS, Rt Rev Samuel.  The Popular and Critical Bible Encyclopaedia. The Howard-Severance Co, 1910.

FAUSSET, A. R.    Bible Dictionary and Encyclopaedia.    Zondervan Publishing House, Grand Rapids, Michigan.

FEDDEN, Robin, Egypt, Land of the Valley. Published by John Murray, 50 Albermarle Street, London, WIX 4BD.  1977

FOX, John. Fox's Book of Martyrs.  Zondervan Publishing House, 5300 Patterson SE, Grand Rapids, Michigan, 49530, 1969.

FOXE, John Foxe's Christian Martyrs of the World. Barbour Books, 164 Mill Street, PO Box 1219, Westwood, New Jersey 07675, 1989.

HALLEY, H.H.    Halley's Bible Handbook.  Published by Zondervan, 1965.

HARRISON, Everett F.   The Apostolic Church.    William B Eerdmans Pub Co, 255 Jefferson Ave, S.E., Grand Rapids, Michigan 49503, 1902, Reprint 1986

HAZARD, Harry W, PhD. Arabian Peninsula. American Geographical Society.  Nelson Doubleday Inc, USA, 1964

HENRY, Matthew & SCOTT, Thomas.   Commentary on the Holy Bible. 3 Volumes, (written 1710 and 1792).   Published by Royal Publishers Inc., Nashville, Tennessee, 1979.

HUNTER, C.F. The New Testament, Its Writers and their Message. Pub J.W. Butcher, Farringdon Street, E.C. London.  1923.

INTERNATIONAL STANDARD BIBLE ENCYCLOPEDIA, Wm B Eerdmans Publishing Co, Grand Rapids, Michigan, USA. 1915, 1989.

JACKSON, F.J. Foakes, DD, The History of the Christian Church from the Earliest times to AD 461. J Hall & Son, Cambridge, 1914.

JEROME and GENNADIUS, (Bethlehem AD 492). Translated by Ernest Cushing Richardson, PhD. Published by James Parker & Co, Oxford, 1892.

JOSEPHUS. Kregel Publications, Grand Rapids, Michigan, 1974.

JOWETT, George F. The Drama of the Lost Disciples. Covenant Publishing Co Ltd. 8 Blades Court, Deodar Road, London, SW15 2NU.

KELLER, Werner. The Bible As History. Hodder and Stoughton, London, 1958.

LATOURETTE, Kenneth Scott. A History of the Expansion of Christianity, Vol 1. Published by Eyre and Spottiswood, London. 1944.

LEWIS, Lionel Smithett, Rev, M.A., Vicar of Glastonbury. St Joseph of Arimathea at Glastonbury. James Clark & Co Ltd, 33 Store Street, London, W.C.1. 1964.

McBIRNIE, William Steuart, PhD. The Search for the Twelve Apostles. Tyndale House Publishers, 336 Gundersen Drive, Wheaton Illinois. 1973.

MORGAN, R.W. St Paul in Britain. Covenant Publishing Co Ltd, 8 Blades Court, Deodar Road, London, SW 15, 2NU. 1948.

MORTON, H. V. In the Steps of the Master. Published by Rich & Cowan Ltd, 25 Soho Square, London. 1934.

MORTON, H. V. In the Steps of St Paul. Published by Rich & Cowan Ltd, 25 Soho Square, London. 1936.

NEWMAN, Dorman. The Lives and Deaths of the Holy Apostles. Kings Arms in the Pountry. 1685

READER'S DIGEST Atlas of the Bible, The Reader's Digest Association Inc, Pleasantville, New York. 1981

RICE, Tamara Talbot. The Early Russians. Frederick Muller Ltd, London, 1963.

SCHAFF, Philip. History of the Christian Church to 1648, in 7 Volumes. This edition 1865.

SCOFIELD, Rev C. I., DD. Scofield Reference Bible & Cyclopaedic Concordance. Oxford University Press. 1945.

SMILEY, David, Arabian Assignment. Leo Cooper, London, 1975.

STOKER, Robert B. The Legacy of Arthur's Chester. Covenant Publishing Co Ltd , 8 Blades Court, Deodar Road, London, SW15 2NU. 1965.

STONEHOUSE, N.B. Origins of the Synoptic Gospels. Baker Book House Grand Rapids, Michigan, 1979.

SUETONIUS. The Tweve Caesars. Translated by Robert Graves. Penguin Books. 27 Wrights Lane, London W8 5TZ, England. 1957

TACITUS. The Annals of Imperial Rome. Translated by Michael Grant. Penguin books, 27 Wrights Lane, LondonW8 5TZ England. 1956

TAYLOR, Gladys. Our Neglected Heritage : The Early Church. Covenant Pub Co Ltd, 8 Blades Court Deodar Road, London SW15 2NU 1969.

TAYLOR, J. W. The Coming of the Saints. Covenant Publishing Co Ltd, 8 Blades Court Deodar Road, London SW15 2NU. 1860, 1948.

THIEDE, Carsten Peter. Jesus - Life or Legend, Lion, Oxford, England 1990.

THIEDE, Carsten Peter and D'ANCONA Matthew. The Jesus Papyrus, Weidenfeld & Nicholson. The Orion Publishing Group Ltd, Orion House, 5 Upper Saint Martin's Lane, London, WC2H 9EA. 1996.

THOMPSON CHAIN REFERENCE EDITION, NIV BIBLE. Hodder and Stoughton, 47 Bedford Square, London WCiB 3DP. 1984.

TISSERANT, Cardinal E. Eastern Christianity in India. Longmans, Green & Co, 6 & 7 Clifford St, London WI, 1957.

TYNDALE NT COMMENTARIES : MATTHEW. Wm B Eerdmans Publishing Co, Grand Rapids, Michigan, 1983.

UNGER, Merril F. Archaeology and the Old Testament. Zondervan. 1964

UNGER, Merril F. Archaeology and the New Testament. Zondervan, 1980.

UNGER, Merril F. Unger's Bible Dictionary. Moody Press, Chicago. 1974

WENHAM, John. Redating Matthew, Mark & Luke. Hodder & Stoughton Ltd., Mill Road, Dunton Green, Sevenoaks, Kent TN132YA, UK. 1991.

LaVergne, TN USA
20 December 2010

209607LV00005B/144/P